On the Edge
The Love/Hate World of the Borderline Personality

by
Neil D. Price, M.D.

19 Prospect Street
Summit, NJ 07901

This book is not intended to replace personal medical care and supervision; there is no substitute for the experience and information that your doctor can provide. Rather, it is our hope that this book will provide additional information to help people understand the complex issues of borderline personality disorder.

Proper medical care should always be tailored to the individual patient. If you read something in this book that seems to conflict with your doctor's instructions, contact your doctor. Your doctor may have medically sound reasons for recommending treatment that may differ from the information presented in this book.

If you have any questions about any treatment in this book, consult your doctor.

In addition, the patient names and cases used in this book do not represent actual people, but are composite cases drawn from several sources.

All rights reserved
Copyright © 1989 The PIA Press

No part of this book may be reproduced or transmitted
in any form or by any means, electronic or mechanical,
including photocopying, recording, or by any information
storage and retrieval system, without permission in writing from
the publisher.
For information address:
Psychiatric Institutes of America,
part of the National Medical Enterprises Specialty Hospital Group.
1010 Wisconsin Ave. NW
Washington, D.C. 20007

Contents

INTRODUCTION 1
CHAPTER ONE: "Borderline According to Whom?" 7
CHAPTER TWO: The Octave of Emotions: Anger,
 Depression, and Then Some 17
CHAPTER THREE: The Making of Borderline Personality
 Disorder 33
CHAPTER FOUR: Attractions Good and Bad 45
CHAPTER FIVE: The Illusion of Relief 53
CHAPTER SIX: Getting Help 70
CHAPTER SEVEN: Safety in Numbers: Group and
 Family Therapy 86
CHAPTER EIGHT: The Proper Use of Medication 95
CHAPTER NINE: When Hospitalization Is Necessary 105
CHAPTER TEN: What Can We Expect? 117
SOURCES 126
INDEX 133

DEDICATION

For my daughters Diana and Pamela, and for my wife, Karen—whom they could depend on.

ACKNOWLEDGMENTS

I wish to thank my teachers in the Department of Psychiatry at Yale University, who taught me how to learn from my patients and how to apply my psychiatric knowledge to best help them.

I would also like to thank Ron Bernstein and Ron Cronen for their encouragement, and Al Smith and Rich Warden for their support.

In addition, I am especially grateful to Rochelle Ratner whose substantial talents were essential to the creation of this book.

Introduction

"Why did you call him?" Angela* screamed at me. "You had no right to tell anyone I was in your office. This is between us." With those words, my telephone line went dead.

A foot-long butcher knife, with which Angela had sliced through the phone wire, was now pointed directly at me.

It was 6:30 now and the clinic was deserted. No one was around to hear what was going on. Angela had moved her chair so that it blocked the door. I was against the far wall, but my office was so small that her knife was only a few inches away from me. For the next hour, Angela sat there threatening to kill me. I deserved to die, she said, since I was "completely rotten and couldn't go unpunished." Every so often she would turn the knife on herself and pierce her bare midriff—enough to cause a little blood, but nothing serious.

As I sat there terrified, desperately trying to think of what to do, I remembered the first time I had met Angela. Angela

---

*All patient names, and their identifying characteristics, have been changed to protect their privacy.

had been a challenge from that very first moment she appeared in my doorway. Six months before, her first words to me had been:

"A Norman Rockwell poster behind your desk? Give me a break," she scowled as she entered. She sat down in the chair and noticed there was dust on the coffee table. For the next half hour she talked nonstop, criticizing my tie, my unshined shoes, the fact that I hadn't bothered to draw the blinds over my window. She talked about Dr. Sherman, her previous therapist, who had graduated and moved to Pennsylvania. "He cared enough about people to buy real art, and *it* was *tasteful*, let me tell you." Her verbal onslaught continued:

"Cat got your tongue, Dr. Freud? Don't you know by now that you're not going to help me that way? You Freudians are all alike: silent, silent, silent."

After a few months of praising her previous psychiatrist and criticizing everything I did or said, Angela began to miss her appointments at the clinic. However, she frequently called me at home. Finally she wrote a letter saying that she no longer wanted me as her doctor. I wrote her a note saying that I was sorry that I couldn't help her, but that if she wished, I would arrange her transfer to another doctor in the clinic. The same day she received my note, she called and booked her old appointment time with me for the next few months.

"You've moved your desk around," Angela said when she showed up on time for her next appointment. "And this is a new picture, isn't it? I like it very much." From that moment on, it seemed I could do no wrong. If I made a comment, she responded with how insightful it was. She began to call me "Dr. Pierce," after her favorite doctor, Hawkeye Pierce from the television show *M*A*S*H*.

Three weeks later Angela called and asked to schedule an emergency appointment. She told me her boyfriend had kicked her out, and that she was alone and frightened. I could hear the anxiety in her voice. I arranged to see her at 6:00 P.M., after my last appointment.

When she arrived at 6:15, Angela screamed, "So what if I'm late, what the hell does it matter? You never gave a damn about me, you were hoping I wouldn't show up. You're just like he was, and I'll bet you're a rotten lover, too, aren't you?" For the next ten minutes she continued to criticize her boyfriend, with innuendos directed at me. This monologue might have continued forever if the phone hadn't rung just then. I excused myself and picked up the receiver. Just as I heard the voice on the other end, the line went dead.

It was at that moment that I found myself facing the butcher knife. I tried to divert her attention.

"Would you have preferred me to wear the checked shirt I had on last time?" I asked, mentioning a shirt she had praised the other day. It was no use; the past was of little concern to her. All that seemed to matter was the moment. Fortunately, as the stalemate continued, her energy slowly dissipated.

"I want to sleep here," Angela said.

"Fine, fine. But you'll be more comfortable with some blankets and a pillow. There are some in the closet down the hall. Would you like me to get them for you?"

Angela yawned and said okay. I slowly walked around her with the point of the knife never more than a few inches from me. I opened the door.

"Come back soon or you'll find me dead!" Angela screamed. "If you're not back in three minutes, I'll kill myself."

I ran out of the building, found a phone, and called the police. Six members of our version of the SWAT team were needed to carry Angela, still raging, out of the building and into the emergency room. "I only wanted us to die together!" she screamed as she was carried past me.

The next time I saw Angela was two days later, in her hospital room. Making sure the nurse's station was alerted to call for help at the first sign of trouble, I sheepishly entered her room to find her sitting up in bed, braiding her long red hair and smiling. "Good morning, Dr. Pierce," she said. Somehow I had become the "good doctor" once again. It was as if the incident the other day had never happened. Angela felt secure and comfortable in the hospital, but was anxious about when she'd be released.

And that's how my fascination with the borderline personality disorder began.

That year was 1982. I was a resident at the Yale University School of Medicine then, working in an outpatient clinic in Connecticut. While "borderline personality disorder" had just been officially recognized as a diagnosis, there hadn't been a movie like *Fatal Attraction* to bring the disorder to national attention. The only thing I knew was that I had never worked with a patient quite like Angela before. For several months after that evening in my office, her case continued to challenge, fascinate, and haunt me.

Angela's chart, thicker than *Gray's Anatomy*, was a sign of how many other residents had struggled with her treatment. Looking it over again after this incident, I was struck by her history of numerous hospitalizations for suicide attempts—superficial cuts on her wrists, pitifully incomplete overdoses. She was an attractive 35-year-old, and her life seemed marked by a succession of unstable relationships.

Everything Angela saw around her was either "all good" or "all bad"; there was no middle ground. Angela had felt somewhat better under her previous psychiatrist's care, and she refused to accept that he had "deserted her." So long as she expected him to return to her, she was forced to ridicule all my attempts to help. It was only when she detected my concern in my note to her (when I said I was sorry things hadn't worked out and offered to help her see another doctor at the clinic) that she began to value my presence in her life.

Her history of relating to other people revealed similar love/hate experiences. She hated her mother, who, she claimed, never paid enough attention to her, but loved her father, who had recently died of cancer. When she was first in treatment with me she was seeing several different men, none of whom were "good enough" for her. Her acceptance of me as a therapist coincided with her forming a live-in relationship with a man twice her age, whom she spoke of interchangeably with her father. As we will see in the pages of this book, nearly all her symptoms fit perfectly into "borderline personality disorder."

In my position as Medical Director of the Tidewater Psychiatric Institute, in Virginia Beach, Virginia, over the past several years, I've had numerous opportunities to work with patients suffering from borderline personality disorder. I've worked with people in private outpatient counseling as well as within the hospital setting. I've tried to help them cope with the crises that mount in their lives from day to day, and to help them restructure their perception of the world around them, and of themselves. I've tried to explain what was going on to concerned relatives and jilted lovers. This book has grown directly out of these experiences.

Some of you may feel that Angela's story is unusual or unique. However, others may be painfully aware of just how common borderline disorder is. The facts can be startling: *About 25 percent of those people today who seek psychiatric help—roughly ten million Americans—have a form of borderline personality disorder.* As recent as thirty years ago, many of these people would have been diagnosed as psychotic or schizophrenic, and thus assumed to be in greater need of hospitalization or intensive treatment than they actually were. Or they would have been termed neurotic or antisocial, and not given as much help as they required.

Understanding what drives the borderline person to act the way he or she does is not a cure-all; it is not even a temporary remedy. But it is a first step. This book presents insights into the turbulent world of the borderline, where everything is either "all good" or "all bad." Beginning with a history of the borderline diagnosis and its evolution within the psychiatric canon, I will discuss the variety of symptoms borderline persons manifest, and how these symptoms vary from those found in both healthy people and in people with more familiar psychiatric disorders. I also comment on how the uncertainties of today's fast-paced world—the dissolution of the nuclear family, the rise in drug abuse and crime, and the increasing number of absentee parents during children's early years—may all be contributing to an increase in borderline personality disorder.

It has been said that there is no such thing as a borderline person who is not receiving help; if he or she does not seek out a professional, help is gained through the nurturance of other people. In the following chapters, I illustrate the ways in which family and friends can help the borderline person to overcome the everyday stresses of our high-paced society, as well as discuss when such efforts may become detrimental and possibly dangerous. In the second half of the book, I examine the various forms of professional treatment available, to assist people in seeking out the advice and assistance they feel will be most useful.

But the person whose life has been touched by the borderline disorder must remember one thing: *There is good news!* For example, even if borderlines do not receive professional treatment, there is a good chance that they will improve as they get older. And with the proper treatment, the borderline person's chances of improvement increase significantly. Researchers and psychiatrists have noted that although the young adult years of borderline persons are often turbulent, a substantial number of them will eventually achieve satisfaction both from employment and interpersonal relationships as they mature. Rough estimates show that 20 to 40 percent of borderline persons who receive psychiatric treatment eventually marry and raise their own families. My own observations clearly indicate that in the majority of cases, the personal relationships of borderline patients improve dramatically with treatment.

If you, or a loved one, suffer from borderline personality disorder, there *is* hope. Read on to find out more about this fascinating disorder: its causes and treatments, plus various strategies for living with it more effectively.

CHAPTER 1

"Borderline According to Whom?"

When my nonpsychiatrist friends hear that I'm writing a book about borderline personality disorder—and once I've given them a brief description of the borderline symptoms—I frequently hear comments like this:

"You know, I have a sister-in-law who fits that woman's description perfectly," one such friend told me over lunch. "I never realized before how sick she was, but now that you mention it..."

Or another friend described an alcoholic coworker in her office: a man who is violent, argumentative, and obscene when drinking, and—when sober—is the nicest guy in the world.

There's only one thing wrong with these examples—in all likelihood, my friends are not describing borderlines.

Most people, the minute they hear descriptions of borderline persons, recognize symptoms in people they know; they may even see the borderline disorder in themselves. However, in most cases, the correct diagnosis of the borderline patient is considerably more difficult.

We must remember that the borderline diagnosis is classified as a *personality disorder*. Like people with other personality disorders—the antisocial, the dependent, the compulsive—the borderline person incorporates traits and attitudes found in all of us, but to a uncontrollable extreme. For example, we are all familiar with the symptoms of a cold, and yet we usually know that these symptoms are not severe enough to be pneumonia. Similarly, we can look at the symptoms of borderline personality disorder and recognize them in friends and associates, but that does not necessarily imply that any or all of their symptoms are severe enough to be termed borderline.

Nevertheless, borderline personality disorder is a very common disorder, one that, historically, has challenged many psychiatrists. How, then, do psychiatrists make a diagnosis? To answer this question, we need to look at borderline personality disorder as it has evolved over the years.

BORDERLINE: A HISTORICAL OVERVIEW

The use and misuse of the term "borderline" in psychiatric literature has been beset with the same turbulence reflected in the borderline person's emotional state. More often than not, the word has had negative, almost frightening connotations: to be on the border of an unspecified mental illness implied to the already anxious patient that she* could easily cross over into some hopeless state. As early as 1884, C. Hughes stated, "The borderland of insanity is occupied by many persons who pass their whole life near that line, sometimes on one side, sometimes on the other." The word

---

*Please note that in order to ease the flow of the text, the female pronoun will be used, unless I am referring to a specific male patient. This is not meant to imply that all persons with borderline personality disorder are female, but merely reflects the fact that the large majority of borderline patients are female.

"borderland" resurfaced in 1919, when L. P. Clark wrote an article for the *Psychoanalytic Review* entitled "Some Practical Remarks Upon the Use of Modified Psychoanalysis in the Treatment of Borderland Neuroses and Psychoses."

It is unfortunate that the term appears nowhere in Freud's writings, although certainly he must have seen patients who would have fit the definition as we understand it today. In 1938, the clinical term "borderline" was first applied to patients, and by 1953 it had become a catch-all or wastebasket term to label patients whose mental states seemed to fall somewhere between neurosis and psychosis. In fact, a common diagnosis of that time—pseudoneurotic schizophrenia—may be what we call borderline today. The rapidly changing symptoms of people given this diagnosis also "bordered" on other conditions, such as manic–depressive disorder, and narcissism. It seemed that any analyst who was presented with a patient with symptoms not fitting into any other category could define her as "borderline" and be done with it.

Without attempting to put a label on the condition he was seeing, Karl Abraham described in 1912 "the depressed person's feelings of inner impoverishment, emptiness, and 'badness,' and inability to love, coupled with the need to project aggression [hate] onto others"—a description that comes much closer to defining the borderline personality disorder as it is understood by psychiatrists and psychologists today. And in 1942, Hermann Rorschach called attention to people who seemed to be functioning adequately in their everyday lives and work situations, but whose responses to his inkblots resembled those given by schizophrenic patients.

Beginning in the mid-1960s, analysts began to use the term "borderline" along the lines suggested by Abraham and Rorschach. But even then, reading these analysts' works, one could come up with a general description of the borderline patient that applied only to some cases, not all. As recently as 1979, at the beginning of my psychiatric residency, whenever a doctor would describe a patient as borderline, the next question would be "borderline according to whom?" Borderline still wasn't a recognized diagnostic category; it was just a collection of thoughts of various people.

Due in large part to the research and interest in the borderline patient during the 1960s and 1970s, Borderline Personality Disorder became a recognizable diagnosis in 1980, when it became part of the DSM-III official diagnostic criteria.

THE TERM TODAY

It's much easier to describe a borderline person's behavior than to pinpoint it diagnostically. To aid in making a diagnosis, psychiatrists often rely on *The Diagnostic and Statistical Manual of Mental Disorders, 3rd Edition, Revised*, or DSM-III-R for short.

The DSM-III-R describes Borderline Personality Disorder as "a pervasive pattern of instability of mood, interpersonal relationships, and self-image." Of the eight possible diagnostic criteria, a diagnosis should not be made until at least five are confirmed:

1. A pattern of unstable and intense interpersonal relationships characterized by alternating between extremes of overidealization and devaluation. (In layman's terms, the borderline patient's view of the other person in relationships flip-flops from either extreme adulation to intense disgust and hatred.)
2. Impulsiveness in at least two areas that are potentially self-damaging, e.g. spending, sex, substance use, shoplifting, reckless driving, binge eating.
3. Affective instability: marked shifts from baseline mood to depression, irritability, or anxiety, usually lasting a few hours and only rarely more than a few days. (In other words, the borderline person suffers from rapidly changing mood swings.)

4. Inappropriate, intense anger or lack of control of anger—e.g., frequent displays of temper, constant anger, recurrent physical fights.
5. Recurrent suicidal threats, gestures, or behavior, or self-mutilating behavior.
6. Marked and persistent identity disturbance manifested by uncertainty about at least two of the following: self-image, sexual orientation, long-term goals or career goals, type of friends desired, preferred values. (Again, in laymen's terms, identity disturbance refers to a person's unstable concept of herself as a human being. It's very common for a borderline patient to say suddenly, "Doctor, I don't know who I am.")
7. Chronic feelings of emptiness or boredom.
8. Frantic efforts to avoid real or imagined abandonment.

We could hardly ask for a clearer description. And yet, on closer examination, we realize that the description is broad enough so that it could include just about anyone. In reality, the case histories of borderline patients illustrate the extremes that typify the borderline's life.

For example, I have one patient, named Jack, who is shy and introverted, and continually moves from one low-paying job to another. In the past, he would use great amounts of alcohol to overcome his feeling of boredom and emptiness, and most times these drunken binges resulted in street fights with anyone he met. The next day, he would feel disgusted with himself, so disgusted that he would punish himself by mutilating his body.

THE "PORCUPINE'S DILEMMA"

Another borderline patient, named Susan, is just entering into treatment. She is a 28-year-old social gadfly: she's always out partying, surrounded by acquaintances she considers close friends, and when she's alone, she constantly has the radio or television blasting to overcome her feelings of despair and depression. She's very quick to hop into bed with both men and women, but no relationship has ever lasted more than a few weeks: she's certain they're not going to love her for very long, and feels she has to leave them before they abandon her, or before she hurts them. This behavior has been characterized as the "porcupine's dilemma": like a porcupine, the borderline wants love and warmth, but is afraid that being close will end in stinging or being stung. In her anxiety about being the first one out of a close relationship, Susan often works herself into a state of anger that ends in physical violence. She goes through long periods of missing her parents desperately, yet the moment they're together she finds herself screaming at them. She has a college degree, yet works as a typist and insists she isn't capable of getting or holding a better job.

Like the rest of humanity, borderline patients come in many different guises. There are those who are introverted and depressed, those who are exhibitionistic and aggressive. While anger is usually present to some extent, some patients direct it only at close friends and relatives, some turn it against anyone they meet, and some only channel it toward self-destruction. But because of the "porcupine's dilemma," *all* borderlines find relationships enormously stressful.

THE ROOTS OF BORDERLINE

As will be explored in Chapter Three, the roots of the borderline personality begin in early childhood, during what has been termed the "rapprochement" phase—16 to 25 months—when the toddler both "shadows" her mother and continually darts away from her; we've all seen this behavior. During this period, it's easy to spot the toddler's need to have the mother close to her, as in her younger months, coupled with her growing fear of becoming too engulfed by the mother's love. The child is thus split into the half that needs and the half that is becoming assertive and anxious for a separate identity; she views the mother as either the good, nurturing mother when the mother is pleasing the child, or the bad mother when she is either absent or engulfing, thus frustrating the child's need to separate. By about the age of 3, this love/fear dilemma usually becomes unified and tempered by the child's growing awareness of her own abilities.

Certainly we all went through that stage of development when we had to deal with a mother who was with us, then left us for brief periods, and we all had to make some sense out of that. We essentially had to do a little *splitting*—we had to do it then, and we have to do it now. By splitting I mean seeing one's mother as all good or all bad. Splitting helps a child deal with the sometimes confusing world of parent-child relationships. To a child, the good and bad sides of a person don't come together, but remain split apart. But when most of us, as adults, lose a person we once cared about, we have enough of a sense of object constancy—the ability to see the good side of someone who has left us or frustrated us. Both the good and the bad memories help us to unify the person into a single, tempered whole.

This is not so in the case of the future borderline personality. It is not so much that the mother is not there at all or does not chase after her sometimes, but that the mother cannot be depended on to do so. The child suffers what we call an exaggerated rapprochement crisis, which will come back to haunt her in later years. Since at that time the mother was still the center of the child's attention, the future borderline child never progresses to the stage where she can perceive, or unify, the "good" mother with the "bad" mother into a single person. Everything in the child's life continues to be seen as "all good" or "all bad"; there are no gray areas.

Having no memory of a whole person to draw upon in later relationships, the borderline person reacts immediately to what is happening. All she feels is pain, and all she sees is that a very negative person has abandoned her. She has no ability to modulate her judgments or restrain her impulsive actions. As Dr. John G. Gunderson has pointed out, the term "borderline" is extremely apt, in that "it reflects the precarious balance of both positive and negative forces in the personality of borderline patients. Their rages and compassions are equally intense." These rages and passions can sit side by side without affecting each other.

In a larger sense, the borderline person is not responding directly to the loss of any one particular person or object. Whatever grief she might feel over a particular loss is experienced instead as continual deprivation, which erupts first in anger, then in helplessness, hopelessness, and self-hate.

THE LARGER PICTURE

The first symptoms of borderline personality disorder usually appear in late adolescence or early adulthood. While I've seen flagrant borderline patients in their fifties and sixties, I think there's a general muting of most personality disorders as people get older. Often a person diagnosed as borderline in late adolescence will exhibit few symptoms by the time she reaches middle age.

Frequently referred to as a condition of "stable instability," borderline personality disorder can be temporarily affected by amounts of stress in the person's day-to-day life, but it generally does not worsen if it is left untreated, and it certainly does not deteriorate into the more serious forms of psychosis, such as schizophrenia. Because of the borderline person's poorly developed self-image, she tends to function best in highly structured situations, whether the structure is provided by another person or by environmental conditions. This is one reason why many borderline patients seek out low-level employment. The person who copes adequately in a clerical position or working on an assembly line might well display an intelligence and aptitude that, if she stays long enough, earns her a promotion. The moment she finds herself in a managerial position, however, she will probably panic and flee, because the added responsibilities bring a lack of structure and new stresses. These new stresses may not only be job-related—an increase in pay may lead to a new home and new economic level.

A large percentage of borderline patients are women. In part, this might be due to the fact that, in today's society, women feel much more at ease in seeking help than do men. Also to be considered here is that women borderlines are more prone to depression and self-mutilation, while men are more frequently found to exhibit symptoms of aggression and loss of control in stressful situations. Whereas a woman might end up hospitalized, a borderline man might find himself in prison.

IS THE BORDERLINE DIAGNOSIS INCREASING?

One thing is certain: the borderline diagnosis has been made with *increasing frequency* over the past two or three decades, and can truly be said to reflect the pressures of modern life. When we take a look around us at the number of single-parent families—mothers working, fathers absent or infrequently available—we can only shudder to think of the number of pre-borderline children we might be raising. A recent study estimated that 65 percent of American mothers work outside of the home, with the majority of their children under 6 years of age. The mothers of 3.7 million infants return to work before the child is 1 year old, according to Nina R. Lief, M.D. Dr. Lief labeled the type of parenting these children receive as "warehouse parenting." *Psychiatric News* quotes Dr. Lief as saying:

"How to obtain proper care for children is a very pressing issue. The solution is not easy. We are the only Western country with no child care policy. Mothers favor government help. They say that as long as men do not personally experience the child care dilemma, the guilt feelings, [and] the frazzled life style that mothers deal with daily, child care options will remain inadequate."

To help solve the problems of warehouse parenting, Dr. Lief recommends that training and salaries for child care workers be increased, and that more parenting groups be established to promote understanding of child development. According to Dr. Lief, "... mothers who understand child development often elect to stay home for the first two to three years of the child's life or work part-time."

Unless some fundamental changes—involving increased funding, education, and training—occur in our society, the borderline personality disorder will continue to plague far too many people.

CHAPTER 2

The Octave of Emotions: Anger, Depression, and Then Some

"You know how children go out for trick or treat on Halloween? Well, when I was little I used to have this trick I always did. I'd bend over so both my head and feet were on the floor, push myself off with my hands and spin. Then I'd pick up my hands and it would just be the head and feet spinning really fast. Well, sometimes I feel like I've never stopped spinning. But nobody's praising me anymore; it just seems as if everyone's angry at me."

—A 30-YEAR-OLD BORDERLINE WOMAN

One patient of mine, named Janice, once called me at 6 P.M. on a Thursday, saying she was feeling more alone and depressed than she had in months; she was frightened that she was going to hurt herself. I arranged an emergency appointment for the next morning, only to have her show up in a state of euphoria about some new man she'd met at a bar the previous night. It was as if our conversation had never occurred. After deeper questioning, I discovered Janice hadn't even spoken to the man; he was just extremely handsome, and she had a feeling he might be interested in her. She was planning to return to the bar in the hope of seeing him again. Not only had the panic and desperation Janice had felt the day before disappeared, but she seemed to have no memory of it.

To go, as Janice did, from depression to euphoria overnight

is typical of the rapid emotional shifts that borderlines display—from love to rage, depression to anxiety, paranoia to utter dependency. These are emotional swings that cannot be influenced by other people.

In a recent article in *American Health,* Dr. Jerold Kreisman aptly refers to borderline persons as suffering from "emotional hemophilia... They lack the clotting mechanism to measure out their spurts of feeling. Stimulate a passion, and they emotionally bleed to death."

The emotional shifts of a borderline are almost always set into motion by some external factor; the person is sometimes, but not always, aware of this precipitating factor. Since the borderline person has little or no sense of individuality, such mood swings appear wholly reliant upon other people, objects, or events that most of us would usually consider insignificant.

As I noted in Chapter One, the borderline person has become deadlocked in a land where there is no gray. Everything, whether internal or external, is experienced in extremes—if something isn't good, then it must be bad. Because Janice was now relating to her "good self," any remnants of the "bad self" had to be completely pushed from her consciousness.

If we take a closer look at this splitting process—a process described briefly in Chapter One—we will get a better understanding of the borderline's storehouse of emotions.

THE ESSENTIAL SPLIT

"I went ice skating last Saturday, and I really couldn't believe how awful it was," a 15-year-old girl told her guidance counselor. "I remember as a little kid I used to love to skate, but I haven't been for a few years. I got out there on the ice and just felt as if everyone was looking at me, waiting for me to fall. I'm certainly not going to be in a hurry to do that again!"

Most healthy people understand, as this girl did, that their identity is not singular, but actually made up of several distinct selves with various needs and desires. Instead of attempting to banish some of these voices, they accept them as a fascinating part of human nature, and value their ability to prefer different things at different times. Because she doesn't enjoy skating as a 15-year-old does not mean she has to invalidate all her happy memories. Neither does it imply that she will always remain in the awkward stage she is currently experiencing. She does not feel threatened by the awareness that she's not the same as she was two years ago.

But the borderline person *does* feel threatened. Her primitive sense of self (or low self-esteem) is neither large enough nor stable enough to contain any contradictions. She feels extremely vulnerable as it is, and cannot permit further conflicts to disrupt her ability to function. By splitting, and moreover banishing any recollection of the self that experienced different feelings, she assumes she is protecting herself. As long as these varied feelings can be kept completely separate, she will feel as if she is "in control." This holds true for her sense of herself, as well as for her perceptions of other people.

When people observe a borderline person in action, they often do not believe their eyes. It seems unfathomable to most people that any one person could move so quickly from one emotional state to its opposite. This again is due to the borderline's ability to split: the "I" who speaks at one moment has no connection with the "I" who speaks the next moment. As Peter Hartocollis has pointed out, within the borderline person, these "I"s "compete among themselves as to which one will begin verbalizing." Often at the beginning of a session there is *silence* as the borderline struggles over who will speak first.

We are all familiar with the temporal nature of the toddler's emotional states: she can give out an agonizing scream if she falls down, but is comforted the minute her mother comes to pick her up. She can act as if the world is coming to an end when she notices that her mother has "abandoned" her, but her attention is quickly drawn to a new toy. This is precisely the process the borderline person goes through as we see her acting out her range of emotions: she is aware only of the here and now. So long as the loved person or object is available, she feels content, but the moment it is taken away, she panics, and acts upon her panic. This panic can be averted only if she ignores, denies, and destroys any memory of the past. Thus, the moment the object is gone from her sight, it becomes "all bad" and therefore unneeded. And since she no longer senses her need, she fails to see how her anger will make matters worse.

Each emotion the borderline person experiences, whether profoundly depressive or vengefully "acting out," is a defensive cover for what she perceives as her internal emptiness, or "badness." Such displays of emotion are thus always more than they appear, and less than they appear.

THE MANY MOODS OF THE BORDERLINE

The borderline person is such a socially motivated creature that it is difficult to conceive of any emotional state as affecting herself alone. More often than not, she is uncertain as to her feelings at a given moment. She would be much more likely to try and figure out how another person is feeling, or to embody that person with the feelings she wishes them to express.

Even when she is depressed or withdrawn, the borderline person is surprisingly receptive to external impressions. But here again, her impressions will quickly revert to fantasies and idealizations. Finding out that the other person does not live up to her expectations, or at best is not as sensitive to her feelings as she assumes she is to his, is viewed as the ultimate rejection, and will usually have traumatic effects.

DEPRESSION

If a therapist asks ten borderline patients how they have felt over the past week, they will probably all answer that they felt depressed. Even though friends and family might have reported various shifts of mood, including some periods of feeling better, all that most borderline patients will recall is the depression. While other people experience transient depression, which under extreme circumstances might continue for some time, the more introverted borderlines use depression as their base state, to which they continually return. Many even respond to actual or imagined abandonment by becoming depressed rather than enraged, but we must remember that such depression can often lead to self-destructive acting out.

While the normally depressed person can usually verbalize longings for a particular object or relationship whose absence has precipitated the depression, the borderline person will deny any such needs even while the cause is clearly visible to a therapist, friend, or family member. Such a depression might at times be accompanied by a sense of hostility at having been deprived or slighted, but the borderline person is unable to pinpoint what or by whom. As she attempts to convey what this depression feels like, she more often appears to be describing boredom, loneliness, or emptiness.

EMPTINESS

Emptiness is the borderline's chronic state, though few people would describe it as such—they'd be more likely to call it depression or boredom. Without another person or object, the borderline has nothing to "fill" her, and experiences only emptiness. Alone, she is incapable of experiencing goals or desires. It might be better described as a feeling of loneliness, except loneliness implies one person longing for a specific person, which is foreign to the borderline's manner of thinking. The borderline does long for something, but cannot identify what this something is.

It is this emptiness that prompts the borderline to be

around other people constantly or, as we saw in one of the patients described in Chapter One, turn to such superficial noise as television or radio when there is no one else around. It is also this state, as we will see in Chapter Four, that causes the borderline person to fill herself with artificial substances such as liquor, drugs, or food—or to slit her wrists to feel the pain.

BOREDOM

Boredom, also experienced by healthy people as a temporary state, can become chronic for the borderline patient. Whereas the borderline calling herself "depressed" will deny any feelings of neediness, the sense of boredom is described by John G. Gunther as: "a sense of longing for something (or someone) that is not merely absent, but nonexistent, or at best unidentifiable, something that leaves one feeling empty or hungry, passively expectant, hopeful in a helpless way." While anger, anxiety, or depression are quickly recognized by other people, the state of boredom often goes unnoticed unless the borderline person expresses it verbally.

I had one borderline patient who was so "bored" that she fell asleep the moment I began to confront her with the fact that she'd been late for her last three appointments. Boredom is often a device used by borderline persons to mask or deny more aggressive feelings. The borderline person in this instance has come to recognize the destructive intensity of her rage, especially toward a valued person or object, and is desperately attempting to control it. Because she has nothing but a sense of depression and emptiness to draw on (the self defined only by the absence of the Other) she has no capacity to replace it with anything other than this neutrality. As long as she is bored (or depressed or empty), the borderline senses herself as protected from feeling, or causing, any greater pain.

ANXIETY

A marked degree of tension, or free-floating (not associated with a specific event or action) anxiety, is frequently observed in borderline persons. It is more often considered either depression or anger, however, since borderlines exist in a timeless realm, acting and reacting only to the present moment. Before one can feel anxious, one must have a well-defined concept of the past and the future. Like boredom, anxiety will often be overshadowed by more conspicuous ailments.

There can be no mistaking that the borderline is continually plagued by separation anxiety—so intensely plagued that at times she becomes wholly unable to function. The moment such anxiety is experienced, however, it is converted into action so quickly that the anxious state itself might well be overlooked. Any indication that her relationship with the person or object on which she has become reliant might be jeopardized stimulates either the extreme depression described above, or any of the acting-out symptoms described in the following.

DENIAL

James F. Masterson, M.D., has pointed out that "it is as if the patient had but two alternatives—either to feel bad and abandoned... or to feel good, at the cost of denial of reality and self-destructive behavior." For the borderline person, denial is the most direct manifestation of the splitting process. She is not as unaware of reality as other people might be led to believe. She might even realize that the impressions about herself or another person that she is expressing at this moment contradict earlier impressions, but since she denies that memory any emotional credibility, it cannot affect her current state. Freed from conflicting emotions, she is once again insulated from stress or anxiety.

DISGUST

Disgust is an emotion frequently expressed by borderline patients, most often in speaking about themselves, and as a reaction to what they view as their essential "badness." Such disgust is often expressed after an "acting-out" episode of self-mutilation, promiscuity, drug or alcohol abuse, binge eating, or irrational spending (see Chapter Four for a longer discussion about these patterns of temporary relief). When initiating such episodes, the borderline does not question their necessity; however, immediately upon return to a supportive environment, such behavior is viewed as shameful, hence her disgust with herself. Sometimes this disgust can be seen as a derivative of depression, sometimes as a derivative of anger, but the central experience of being "all bad" is the same in either case.

DISSOCIATED SPEECH PATTERNS

"It was such a nice day today we bundled up and went for a walk. Believe it or not, we ran into Barbara. We went to lunch at Golden's, and boy, was she restless and mad, she took forever serving us, I don't understand what we did to anger her. Then we came home and had dessert and coffee. We're having chicken for dinner, can you still smell it?"

When the husband of this woman heard these comments, he at first didn't know what to make of them. On questioning her further, he realized that his wife had taken their baby daughter for a walk and run into her friend Barbara. The three of them had gone to lunch together, the baby was restless and mad, and it was the waitress who took forever serving them, and whom his wife had also perceived as angry. His wife, the baby, and Barbara had come back to the house for dessert and coffee, but he was the "we" referred to as having chicken for dinner. The "it" she was asking if he could still smell was not the chicken, but a pie she had put in the oven earlier.

Andre Green has pointed out that "the discourse of the borderline is not a chain of words, representations, or affects, but rather—like a pearl necklace without a string—words, representations, affects contiguous in space and time but not in meaning. It is up to the observer to establish the missing links with his own psychic apparatus." In part due to the fact that her own sense of self is continually changing, the borderline will see no difficulty in continually referring to a changing use of "we." As in the case of the woman who took it for granted that the waitress was slow because she was angry, the borderline will tend to elaborate or impose too many false perceptions on other people as she describes the events of a day. While those to whom she is talking might well understand and accept the basic premise of what is being said, the reasoning is often difficult to understand and, even once understood, felt to be mistaken.

Such dissociative speech patterns also facilitate regression into fantasy, permitting the borderline person to include other people in a nonexistent "we."

OUTWARDLY DIRECTED AFFECTS

"I'd been dating Dara steadily for about six weeks, and I thought things were going great. Then my sister called to say she was coming in town. I hadn't seen her in three years, and I suggested to Dara that, the first night, it might be best if I saw my sister alone. Dara started crying about how I was too ashamed of her to introduce her to my family. Then she accused me of having an incestuous relationship with my sister, called me a pervert, and stormed out of the restaurant. It wasn't as if I was saying she'd never meet my sister, for God's sake. All I wanted was one night alone. There was no way I could understand Dara's reaction."

The borderline is constantly responding to external objects, so much so that even her depressions embody feelings of helplessness, hostility, injustice, and having been deprived of her rights. As has been noted, all her actions are both impulsive and defensive. We need only to recall the momentary and momentous temper tantrums of the toddler to get a clear picture of such states.

While acting-out gestures such as suicide attempts and substance abuse are not discussed here (see Chapter Four), the borderline's more direct attacks and accusations, as well as her frequent explosions into anger and less-frequent psychotic episodes, require examination. Bear in mind that this is once again the dilemma of the rapprochement phase: desiring the close relationship with the mother or other person vs. feeling herself engulfed by it. The following outwardly directed affects can be motivated by illusions of either need or entrapment.

SARCASM, HOSTILITY, DEVALUATION, ETC.

The borderline person has an extremely low tolerance for frustration, and is quick to assume that a minor sign of irritation means she is "all bad" and the person she is reliant upon is about to leave her. When she first becomes anxious regarding a real or imagined threat of abandonment, the outward expression will often take such fairly mild forms as sarcasm, being demanding, unreasonable, and argumentative, impatience, bitterness, and irritability—affects that might only be recognized by other people in retrospect. At this point, her emotions are still held in check because the needed person or object retains its original value, and whatever her anxieties, she is still in fear of losing it. The moment she senses she is losing her ability to hold this object, the process of devaluation or outright hostility frequently begins. Such actions are still manipulative, conscious efforts to regain control over the object.

ANGER

Depression (or emptiness) might well be the emotion that the person with borderline personality disorder considers herself to feel most of the time, but anger is what she most often expresses to others. "Anger" as I am using it here has many implications, including anger at oneself, well-founded anger at other people, irrational attacks on people who are only trying to be of help, and all-inclusive rages at any person or object that crosses her path.

At times, anger can be used in the same manner as the acting-out symptoms discussed in Chapter Four are used—as a means to fill the emptiness. Thus the borderline person in a severely depressed or bored state might well become angry or provoke anger in others as she attempts to regain a lacking sense of identity. At such times, she often retains the sense of the other person's importance, in essence minimizing the effect of splitting. Recovering from such an emotional outburst, she once again sees herself as "all bad" and will often experience the disgust referred to previously.

The knowledge that the other person is loved and valued is similarly maintained when the outburst is more defensive and manipulative in nature, responding to a real or imagined threat of abandonment or rejection. But no matter how distorted her original perceptions might have been, so long as the cause of her anger is viewed by her as having been provoked, it will not be regretted later.

When it comes right down to it, borderlines are more likely to turn their anger against themselves, as evidenced by their frequent and manipulative suicide attempts. But they're also prone to horrible, pathological jealousy, and when they become involved in a relationship, they are more than capable of doing harm to the person they're most angry with.

It should be stressed once again that milder forms of manipulation frequently precede outbursts of rage. It is only when all else fails that the object or person becomes split into "all bad" and the real anger erupts. The problem is that it is often like watching a movie played at fast-forward speed: the borderline person progresses from one state to the next so quickly that we fail to recognize the intermediate steps.

TWILIGHT STATES

The person with borderline personality disorder is quick to flee from any stressful, confrontational situation. At times such a "flight" can take the form of brief memory lapses, fugue-like dissociative states, and actual amnesia. Considering the borderline's poorly developed sense of identity to begin with, it is not surprising that she should be prone to such states, which are often considered to be prepsychotic experiences.

BRIEF PSYCHOTIC EPISODES

The presence of psychotic episodes does not appear in the diagnostic criteria for borderline personality disorder, and there are some clinicians who argue that this is a rarely discovered symptom in borderline patients. I disagree—psychotic episodes can occur often. They might be extremely brief, but they are frequently experienced, particularly by those persons who have not entered into a therapeutic relationship, and are often what prompts them to seek out professional treatment. Once they have entered treatment, the support that the borderline patient senses from the therapist as a Significant Other often greatly diminishes the frequency with which such episodes occur.

A distinction must be made here between the true psychotic episode—which implies a total loss of one's grasp of reality, however brief—and the common trait of the person with borderline personality disorder to project her feelings onto another person. I have had many patients scream at me for being so angry at them, when in fact they were the only ones expressing any anger. Such a patient has not lost her grasp on reality; it is simply that her poorly developed sense of self and her need to protect herself from feeling "all bad" permits her to more easily project such "badness" onto others.

Once again, even major psychotic episodes must be viewed within the perspective of the borderline person's great need to have other people around in order to prevent the dreaded emptiness within. Other borderline symptoms, such as depression, devaluation, and anger, will almost always precede any psychotic episode, and it can be postulated that the episode itself is a last resort to avoid the feeling of being alone with herself. While the preceding symptoms are often manipulative, the psychotic episode indicates that all sense of reality is lost—including attempts to control reality. There is no such thing as manipulation at this point.

At times a psychotic episode might be triggered by anger that has become so intense as to become frightening to the borderline person herself. In such instances, it might be viewed as the only way out, as well as a warding off of "total badness." At other times it might be in response to the actual loss (by death or divorce) or a person she felt necessary to her existence (such as a therapist, doctor, spouse, or friend.

So long as what the borderline views as a supportive, needed relationship remains unthreatened, her sense of reality is also secure. When the relationship becomes endangered, her immediate perception of reality might waver and become distorted, but the ability to test reality remains intact. When actual loss occurs or is thought to have occurred, there are times when the borderline's hold on reality simply becomes too much to tolerate, and a psychotic episode ensues. What is remarkable, however, is how quickly the sense of reality returns the moment that there is the renewed presence of a support network, whether provided by a family member, a therapist, or a hospital.

Obviously, these categories only begin to touch on the full gamut of the borderline's emotional displays. Such affects as jealousy, envy, euphoria, a sense of futility, frustration, and confusion might easily be added. It would be safe to say that any emotion we see in another person might be seen in its most extreme form in a borderline person.

TO AVOID CONFUSION

Considering that borderline personality disorder was not a recognized diagnostic criterion until 1980, it should come as no surprise that health professionals and the general public alike frequently mistake the symptoms of the borderline person with symptoms of other psychological disorders with which they are more familiar. If one meets a borderline person at a point when she is experiencing her own emptiness and badness, she might be mistaken for a depressed person; if one meets her during a brief psychotic episode, she might be mistaken for a schizophrenic. While the actual symptoms and emotional states of borderline personality disorder are so diverse that even attempts to explain them can add to the confusion, it will help if we distinguish the borderline symptoms from the more prevalent variations found in other people.

The depressed person might experience a high degree of guilt, but she will still maintain a fairly balanced view of herself. Because the depressed borderline sees herself as "all bad," she is unable to respond to reasoned attempts to alleviate the depression, and is much more likely to become impulsively self-destructive. Though one might find the borderline crying or unable to sleep during periods of intense depression, such periods are seldom accompanied by the loss of appetite or weight loss seen in other chronically depressed persons. The depressed person often cannot experience pleasure, but the borderline, while she can be unhappy, often can experience moments of happiness.

The antisocial person does not care what other people think of her and can shamelessly exploit all the people around her. The borderline person, on the other hand, becomes manipulative and exploitative when she has been disappointed or frustrated by the other person's failure to live up to her high expectations. In addition, the antisocial person can be very charming as a means of exploiting someone, but the borderline is usually not likeable.

The neurotic person frequently displays many of the socially unacceptable affects of the borderline, but she does not have a history of self-destructive behavior, drug abuse, and suicide attempts, nor does she express the intense need to manipulate and devaluate her close friends and relatives. The defensive actions taken by the neurotic are reasoned and repressive in nature; those taken by the borderline are impulsive and primitive.

The histrionic person is concerned with getting other people to take responsibility for her actions, and may resort to manipulation in order to achieve her goals, but her actions are again less frequently self-destructive. The histrionic person is capable of sustaining a relationship, and is less likely to idealize people she feels are important to her. There is usually not the same degree of anger in her basic nature, and she might well experience sustained periods of contentment. Also, the histrionic person is often quite seductive, a trait less often seen in the borderline.

The narcissistic person has an inflated, omnipotent view of herself, and continually requires the admiration of other people. The narcissistic person will flee from criticism to find flattery. Conversely, the borderline person has an inherent sense of her own "badness" and needs other people around her to prevent the panic she experiences when she is alone. Rather than admiration, the borderline yearns for nurturance. Thus the narcissistic person can present herself to others with a degree of detachment of which the borderline person is not capable. The narcissistic person may experience feelings of inferiority when other people do not respond as she would hope, but she will see this as due to the envy or stupidity of other people, rather than to her own "badness."

The schizophrenic person, far less dependent upon other people, is thus less manipulative. Where the borderline person is quick to anger, the schizophrenic would be quicker to remove herself from the frustrating situation. She is more often found to be a "loner," has often all but given up the desire to be seen in a social situation, and the quality of her close relationships will never reach the intensity that is the borderline's mainstay. While the borderline might feel powerless to change her patterns of relating to others, she has not given up hope of a sustained relationship, as the schizophrenic often has. Under most circumstances, the borderline person will remain conscious of the other person's needs and desires, and retain a general awareness of reality even if she is not admitting it to herself.

As mentioned above, the psychotic episodes of the borderline person are generally less severe than those of the schizophrenic, and the borderline person does not have the ability to sustain such episodes, but will revert to relative normality the moment she feels herself in a supportive environment.

CHAPTER 3

The Making of Borderline Personality Disorder

"Walk by yourself," I heard a mother scream at her toddler in the mall last weekend. "You didn't want to hold my hand a minute ago, well you can just manage on your own now." The child waddled along a few steps behind, crying, reaching her arm out to thin air.

This woman wasn't what most of us would think of as a "bad" mother. She was angry, and felt as if she had a right to be angry. We were in a mall, so there was no chance of the child darting out into the street and being hit by a car. She had an infant in a carriage and a slightly older child to think of as well. Besides, I could see her keeping her eye on her daughter even while she pretended to ignore her.

Yet I was tempted to stop the mother and warn her of the harm she might be doing. I kept seeing the possibility of borderline personality disorder in the making.

I was, of course, overreacting to the immediate scene. Certainly I know as well as anyone that it takes more than one such incident to cause later problems in a child's development. A personality or personality disorder is not molded by any one experience, but by the repeated cycle of our wishes being either fulfilled or deprived. And even so, this will be but one among many factors, including a biologically influenced threshold for stress. The healthy person learns to accept what cannot be given and finds ways to cope as best she can with what is made available.

We have all seen one or two of those infants who are a pleasure to be around. Almost immediately they manage to sleep through most nights, and even when they wake up hungry they are easily fed and comforted. They might curl up with a stuffed animal in the crib, but when they are half asleep, the animal can be removed without their paying any attention. Such children have an innate ability to tolerate minor frustrations. Then there is the other child, possibly a sister or brother to this one, who finds it impossible to get back to sleep once she has been awakened, and very seldom sleeps through a night. Move the blankets to cover her better when she is half asleep and she will wake up crying and flailing her arms in the air.

While a genetic inability to tolerate frustration is often present from birth in people with borderline personality disorder, this does not mean to imply that every infant who has trouble sleeping or is not easily pacified will grow up to exhibit borderline symptoms. The future borderline will not have the natural resources to compensate for early "traumatic" experiences, making her excessively susceptible to problems in her later development. But even given these inherent defects, if such a child receives an abundance of care and nurturing during her first three years of life, more often than not later psychological problems can be avoided. It is only when genetic factors are combined with a mother who is not available enough, or whose availability cannot be depended upon, that developmental problems might arise.

Freud, in perhaps too militaristic a description, stated that we all start off life with a certain amount of "armies." After each phase of development, we lose some of our armies. Of course we all lose some armies, but if too many are lost at one particular stage, then we end up having a particular set of problems.

NORMAL INFANCY

The newborn infant has no concept of her existence being separate from her mother. When such a child is held, she simply molds herself to her mother's body. Her cry of hunger will seem to emanate from the same source that immediately responds to the cry with the needed nourishment. The coughing or burping by which the infant is made to feel more comfortable is not differentiated from the mother's changing of her position or putting on a clean diaper, which has a similar comforting effect. Within the first few weeks of life, she will distinguish between the "bad" or painful experience of hunger and the "good" or comforting experience of being fed, but still see both the need and the fulfillment as coming from the same source.

Gradually the infant begins to look around her, to respond more to the environment, and to perceive herself as a being apart from her mother. In their groundbreaking book, *The Psychological Birth of the Human Infant*, Margaret S. Mahler, Fred Pine and Anni Bergman observe this process "in such behavior on the part of the infant as pulling at the mother's hair, ears, or nose, putting food into the mother's mouth, and straining his body away from the mother in order to have a better look at her, to scan her and the environment." This period, from 5 to 30 months, has been referred to as the "separation-individuation" phase of development.

THE PRACTICING PHASE

True to its name, the "practicing phase" of development—roughly 8 to 16 months—is when the toddler practices her ability to function alone. As soon as the child is physically able to begin to get around on her own, the outside world draws her attention. She might struggle to get off her mother's lap, but most often stays and plays as nearby as possible. As the child's understanding of her own individuality increases, she begins to venture farther away. The external surroundings absorb her for longer and longer periods.

She begins to differentiate between good and bad (pleasurable and painful) images of her mother, and later carries these associations forward to other aspects of her environment. As long as the mother is nearby, the child will show an increasing interest in strangers. Her explorations at this point are still tentative, however. While she views her own accomplishments as grandiose, she is in need of her mother's reassurance and approval if she is to continue to accept them as such. As Dr. James F. Masterson has pointed out, if the child's psychological development is arrested during this practicing stage, there is a good chance that the evolving person will be extremely narcissistic—although the toddler can physically move away from the mother, the child still carries "Mom" in her head.

THE RAPPROCHEMENT PHASE

The rapprochement (from the French word for "peacemaking" or "coming together") phase is the key to understanding the borderline personality disorder. During this phase, from 16 to 25 months, the child becomes aware of her presence as separate and distinct from her mother. Mother is no longer an extension of the child, a comforting force that feeds, changes the diaper, or holds the new toy. The child no longer turns to her mother simply for acknowledgment and approval—she needs a mother who will *share* the toy, not simply hold it. She has discovered that her mother is a person, too. Moreover, she is starting to realize that her own concept of enjoyment, her own wants and needs and desires, might be different from her mother's. This realization brings added anxiety to the child.

Not only does the child now know herself to be separate, but she also experiences loneliness, helplessness, and anxiety. Such fears are a normal part of growing up. Learning how to cope with this anxiety is the most important aspect of the rapprochement stage of development. Assuming that the child's previous association with her mother has been productive, and that the child has not previously displayed an inability to tolerate frustration, there should be no major problems at this point.

It is also at about 18 months of age that the child gains the ability to remember people and objects when they are not physically present. It is this newfound skill which, as we saw in Chapter One, gives the child the courage to "dart away" from her mother and assume that mother will be there to sweep her up in her arms once again. Or, during less courageous moments, the child will shadow her mother to make certain of her presence.

But what happens when mother is not physically present? At the start of the rapprochement phase, the child seems to retain a vague, somewhat incomplete memory of her. Most children, as the rapprochement phase progresses, are able to turn their attention to other children, adults, or games in which they fantasize their mother's presence. One child in Mahler's study, for example, played with a ball which was continually "lost" and "found" again, thus tempering the reality of separation.

Some children obviously become more anxious than others at the thought of their mother's leaving. At this stage in life, the anxiety is expressed in aggressive behavior. But aggression can take many different forms. Margaret S. Mahler, M.D., reported that, if a child had made desperate attempts to prevent her mother's departure, she might respond to her return with indifference or even a failure to recognize her. This can be better understood if we return to the concept of "splitting" described in Chapter Two. The child recognized her own aggression, and also saw that it did not prevent her mother from leaving. She therefore came to see herself as a "bad" child abandoned by a mother who had every right to be angry. Moreover, since her memory of her mother is vague and incomplete, it is easy for the child to "forget" the "good" mother and the good times they shared. Thus, her momentary inability to recognize her mother upon return. Forgetting the "good" mother also "protected" her from the "bad" child's anger and aggression.

Most children learn to cope well with their separate identity somewhere between their second and third year of life. Before this can be accomplished, the child must be able to retain a positive, unified image of her mother, or any other necessary object or person. Mother might leave, and the child might miss her, but she will not reject or "forget" her mother simply because she is not present to satisfy her needs. Instead of feeling defeated by external sources, she can maintain a comforting image of her mother. She is not afraid to acknowledge her own angry feelings. Instead of seeing everything as necessarily "good" or "bad," "loved" or "hated," the child learns to channel her aggression toward building a positive image of herself as an individual. She no longer needs to fantasize or deny her own separate existence.

"GOOD-ENOUGH" PARENTING

Otto F. Kernberg, M.D., is emphatic in stating that children need the maximum availability of their mothers during the first 24 months of life. If for some reason the mother becomes unavailable over an extended period of time, an exaggeration of the rapprochement crisis might result. If we add to this an absent or emotionally unavailable father, and a

The Making of Borderline Personality Disorder ■ 39

child whose own resources are vulnerable and unstable, borderline symptoms might well appear in later years.

The question as to what factors might cause the mother's "unavailability" remains the major issue here. Obviously, death or divorce during this period could prove traumatic to the child. Most borderline persons, however, were raised by their natural mothers, so we must look further for answers (see Chapter One).

As we discussed, during the first few months of her life, the infant assumes that her mother is an extension of herself. Even as she begins to differentiate between herself and her mother, her need for her mother's continual presence cannot be questioned.

As the child's physical skills increase, she becomes curious and anxious to explore on her own. When her interests are drawn to something in the environment, she can at times seem almost unaware of her mother's presence. As Edward R. Shapiro has stated, during this period the mother must be able to "tolerate sufficiently her own wishes for dependency and autonomy so that she can respond in a stable emphatic way to corresponding wishes in her child without seeing them as 'bad' or dangers and responding with retaliation or withdrawal." As that woman with her children in the mall made all too clear to me, not all mothers are capable of doing this.

Even the best of mothers will at times respond abruptly or "wrongly." The "good-enough" mother is not afraid of anger, whether her own or her child's. Because she understands the human capacity to both hurt and recover from hurt, she can be strict with her child without fear of causing permanent damage. She can be sensitive and show how much she cares for the child at the same time that she is angrily responding to one act. As Mahler's study proves, there is an enormous range for action and reaction within the "good-enough" spectrum.

For some women, problems arise the moment the child shows independence. These women place too high a value upon the knowledge that they are the only person who can satisfy the child's needs. Such a mother feels additional conflict as the infant begins to assert herself. Subconsciously, she makes herself responsive and available to the child as long as the child continues to cling to her. When the child attempts to venture forth on her own, the mother emotionally removes herself. James F. Masterson expresses it best when he says, "The child needs the mother's supplies in order to grow; if she grows, however, they are withdrawn from her..."

The child gets the impression that "If I grow up, I'll be all alone in the world." She doesn't want to grow, at the same time that she feels the need to explore because she *is* growing. She becomes more and more anxious. When her mother is around, she clings; when her mother is not around, her aggression seems unbounded. Life becomes a constant struggle.

Unable to unify the presence of the "good mother" with the rage at the "bad mother" who has abandoned her, the child develops the first stages of borderline personality disorder. And since her mother is her first and most important figure to exist outside herself, she's subsequently unable to reconcile the good and bad in herself and other people. Because her aggression, or "badness," has had no outlet, she views only its destructive aspects, and lives in fear of letting other people see them as well—the "porcupine's dilemma" described in Chapter One.

Some authors have suggested that the mother of the future borderline might well be borderline herself. While I think this might be an exaggeration, it is certain that many mothers of borderlines have problems with relationships. Such a mother cannot permit her child to become a separate person, for fear that this would leave her alone, yet she is also afraid of letting the child become too close to her. It is not that the mother wants to deprive her child; it is often that she doesn't know how else to respond. Many such mothers were denied a crucial amount of nurturing in their own childhoods: this clinging child thus makes her uneasy and impatient, yet the child coping on her own is unbearable.

ADOLESCENCE: THE CONFLICT REPLAYED

I met Barbara, a very quiet, shy 15-year-old, my first year at Tidewater Psychiatric Institute. She was hospitalized after slitting her wrists in the high school parking lot during a dance. She'd used her boyfriend's penknife to make the cut, but was brought to the emergency room by two girlfriends. The boyfriend had told her he'd "had enough of her stupid tantrums" and walked away.

It seemed like a rather familiar story—the girl is jilted by her lover and slits her wrists. Except her friends told me Barbara slit her wrists *before* the boy had walked away. She also impressed me as too sullen and intelligent a girl to have pulled such a stunt just to get attention. Her school records reported quite a few problems in kindergarten and first grade—daydreaming and being prone to tantrums when she didn't get her way—but she hadn't been a discipline problem since second grade.

Barbara was quick to volunteer the information that her parents hadn't wanted her to go to the dance. But then she corrected herself: her father said it was fine if she went; her mother was the one who insisted she was too young. The rest of the story I had to learn in small pieces. Barbara had gone into a tantrum, which merely confirmed her mother's opinion. The father then proceeded to taunt the mother. By that time, Barbara had no choice but to go to the dance. Otherwise her father would turn his anger on her, and the whole family would spend the next week not speaking to each other. Even so, she'd made her boyfriend promise to have her home by 11:30 because, as she put it, "I was worried about my mother going crazy."

At 11:20, her boyfriend refused to leave. Barbara first tried to cajole him. She then began to threaten and cry, but it didn't do any good. All she could think of was that her mother was probably at home hysterical. Barbara didn't want her parents to fight again, especially over her. She thought maybe if she did something like slit her wrists it would make them both rush to her aid and everything would be fine again. She seemed to have no awareness that the incident could possibly cause her any harm. Or, when I insisted upon pointing possible implications out to her, she stated flatly that it would still be preferable to the alternative effect of her parents getting so angry at each other.

During the first few days Barbara was hospitalized, her mother was with her almost constantly, neglecting both her husband and her two other children. Barbara talked continually about not wanting her mother to "baby me this way," yet the moment her mother left she was observed by staff to become extremely anxious.

Leading developmental child psychologist Erik Erikson describes how a person's quest for self-discovery, which begins in the rapprochement stage of development, culminates in adolescence when "the adolescent must test, select, and integrate the self-images derived from the psychosocial crises of childhood in the light of the ideological climate of youth. In their search for a new sense of continuity and sameness which must now include sexual maturity, adolescents must come to grips again with the crises of earlier years before they can extol lasting idols and ideals as guardians of the final identity." Or, to put this concept into its most simplistic form: During adolescence, the child must once again break away from her parents' values, wants, and needs. She again explores her environment in order to find her own place in the scheme of things. It is the rapprochement crisis played over almost line for line, but this time with a child who, if her aggression has never been moderated, is capable of doing both herself and other people significant harm.

Once the picture of Barbara's early childhood became clear,

it was easy to see how these never-resolved separation conflicts were bound to cause problems. As in many families of borderline teenagers, Barbara's mother seemed able to function well in her day-to-day life, and had permitted her two other children a normal growth pattern. Barbara was her youngest child, literally her mother's "last hope." Now that Barbara was desirous of her individuality once again, her mother had no choice but to withdraw whatever support and encouragement she'd previously managed to give.

Meanwhile, Barbara's inability to set out on her own as a small child had resulted in a shy, quiet girl who had few close friends; thus she was often around the house, keeping her mother company in the absence of her father and the other children. She and her mother would go to the movies together on Saturdays. Together they went on shopping sprees and to lunch in excellent restaurants. Barbara had a deep, inbred anxiety that if she left, the entire family would fall apart and, what's more, she was probably right.

Barbara also knew how fragile she herself was. She felt that she wouldn't be able to function well if she were completely alone, so therefore she wanted to do everything to make sure the family remained together. She was convinced that it had been her own "badness" that had prevented her from making friends throughout childhood—if she'd been "good," everyone would like her, and she was certain she wouldn't feel so dependent on her family.

Many children who suffer pre-borderline symptoms during early childhood do not show any symptoms during the early school years (the "latency" period, roughly 6 to 10 years of age); however, they become overwhelmed once again as they enter adolescence. Traditionally, psychiatrists and psychologists have been reluctant to acknowledge the severity of maladaptive symptoms displayed by adolescents, regarding even minor suicide attempts as a necessary part of the growing process. Despite such optimism, follow-up studies with adolescents diagnosed as having specific psychological problems have proved that these problems persist almost unchanged well into adulthood.

Treatment for adolescents as well as adults with borderline personality disorder will be explored in the second half of this book. I want to point out here, however, how important it is that when a borderline adolescent has her first break, her first obvious self-destructive act which brings her to everyone's attention, a period of hospitalization is almost a necessity. As in Barbara's case, the entire family is united to deny the patient's symptoms, and a lot of that denial is broken down by the significance of having an adolescent in the hospital. Unless the entire family is engaged in the therapeutic process, where the patient can be observed in her day-to-day interactions with other family members, there is little hope of making much progress.

CHAPTER 4

Attractions Good and Bad

One of our most popular songs refers to "people who need people," considering them to be "the luckiest people in the world." It is a song we can all relate too—certainly we have all felt vulnerable at one time or another and experienced that desperate need to have other people close to us, to be assured that we are cared for so that we can function better in the other aspects of our lives.

As we usually apply the word "need" in this context, we are conveying how much we enjoy spending time with friends and family. We have noticed that a friend's unexpected visit or phone call enables us to feel better when in a bad mood. And when we are with friends, we can relax and enjoy the time together, without becoming obsessed that friends are going to leave us. In describing ourselves as "needing" other people, we seldom have the borderline personality in mind. But to a borderline, the term "needing" has a different context.

THE ADULT CHILD

If we return for a moment to the case of Angela, presented in the Introduction, we will be able to get a clearer picture of how the adult with borderline personality disorder exhibits all the symptoms of the child locked in the rapprochement stage of development. During the early stages of treatment, Angela's missed appointments, followed by attempts to call me on the phone mimicked the "shadowing" behavior of the child insecure about her mother's continued presence. Her shadowing of me could be seen as both a wish for reunion and a fear of engulfment.

Angela writing to say she no longer wanted me as her doctor, then booking several appointments after my compassionate response, could be described as a type of "darting away" behavior also characteristic of the same period. Clearly she expected to be swept up in my arms, and felt her expectations fulfilled, as was evident in the change in the therapeutic relationship from this point on. She was still going through the process of "splitting," but now I was the "good" therapist, while her previous therapist became the "bad" therapist. Her idealization of me (and her inability to see me as a real, individual person) was further evident in her referring to me as "Dr. Pierce." Similarly, her parents had been neatly divided into the "all good" father and the "all bad" mother. Even the words she applied as she described her parents recalled the anxious, frustrated child. More often than not, they sounded like caricatures rather than real people.

Robert J. Waldinger, describing the fantasies created by children to protect themselves from their experiences of aggression, writes in the *American Journal of Psychiatry* about how the child "mobilizes primitive defenses to extricate himself or herself from the threatening interpersonal relationships and thus creates 'monsters,' where in reality only imperfect parents exist." However real such monsters might have been, they did not give an accurate picture of Angela's family structure.

Smooth, consistent development from infancy through childhood and adolescence into a mature individual with a well-developed and secure personality structure is difficult even under the best of circumstances. The fast-paced society of the past three decades has been extremely hostile to human growth, and we can only marvel at the resiliency of those persons who manage to overcome all obstacles. But the borderline individual, as discussed in Chapter Three, was not overly well endowed with the resources necessary to succeed against all odds.

As a result of what has been termed the "push-pull" struggles with her mother during infancy, the growing child loses herself in fantasy. At first forced to deny only the reality of her separate existence, her fantasies of reunion with her mother (or any other object or person she deems necessary) take over her being to the point where she no longer has the ability to differentiate between what is real and what is not.

Angela's entire life had been arranged in terms of pleasing some "all good or all bad other person"—whether her mother, her father, Dr. Sherman, her boyfriend, or myself. Unable to sense her separate existence, she had to become fused with another person so that, as G. J. Sarwer-Foner has explained, "the other person plus the patient form a whole." At no point did Angela see any of these other people as they actually were. Projecting her own wishes onto them, she was able to idealize them. They would both protect and nurture her. Her memories of being cared for by her mother as long as she was a submissive child were never far from her consciousness, and this knowledge prevented her from taking a mature stance in any of her later relationships. The moment she felt threatened by abandonment, she regressed to childish, impulsive behavior. And if this didn't work, both the other person and herself became "completely rotten" people who "couldn't go unpunished." She fantasized death as an escape from her own rottenness, still having no sense of its reality or finality.

FATAL ATTRACTION

I am no longer the young resident working with his first borderline case, yet Angela's threatening butcher knife only a few inches from my chest continues to haunt me. When I was originally planning this book, I thought about citing a group of people for whom relationships were more dangerous than for other people. All I could focus on was how perilous life is for those people who become involved with borderlines.

Two years ago, the movie *Fatal Attraction* was instrumental in driving this point home to the general public. Dan's wife and daughter are away for the weekend; Dan (played by Michael Douglas) stays in Manhattan for a business meeting. At the meeting he encounters Alex (Glenn Close), an attractive young editor he'd met briefly at a party the night before. They spend the night together. Dan leaves early the next morning, but Alex calls and convinces him to return. They spend the day in bed, he gets up to go home, she screams not to leave, then slits her wrists. Dan bandages her wrists and stays. He assumes it's over after the weekend, but she won't let him alone—calls at the office, calls to his house at all hours (hanging up when his wife answers). He agrees to see her just to tell her to stop; when they meet, her first comment is, "I knew you'd never leave me." From that point on, Alex's attacks assume increased violence in an effort to regain Dan's love—blowing up his car, killing his daughter's pet rabbit, and finally attempting to kill his wife and getting killed herself in the act.

On the one hand, Alex has a clear conception of reality: she knows Dan is married, that this is only a brief affair. On the other hand, she finds it impossible to accept this fact, and gradually becomes more and more psychotic. The ending, I admit, is too dramatic, and betrays the Hollywood attempt to produce a thriller. But throughout the first half of the movie, Alex's actions are so typical of borderline personality disorder that I sometimes felt as if I were watching one of my patients up there on the screen.

In October 1987, a few weeks after the film appeared, *People* magazine did a cover story on "Real-Life Fatal Attractions." At the start of the article, it was noted that casual conversations about the film "tends to provoke startling confessions from both men and women that begin: 'Something like that happened to me...'" The article went on to report several "real-life" cases—a woman kidnapped by a former lover, cars blown up, wardrobes slashed, a new bicycle sent to the son of a one-night stand. We can pick up a newspaper on just about any given day and read similar stories. Usually, though, we only read about the more dramatic cases, the murders and suicides. We don't hear about the phone calls made in the middle of the night, the person who breaks the windows of his lover's house, the man who returns to his desk after lunch to find his papers shredded. One of the reasons the film proved so successful was because it struck a familiar chord in all of us.

BRIEF INFATUATION

Someone once said that the ideal relationship for borderlines was a weekend: it provided a way to get out before getting hurt. Borderlines are capable of falling in love, but not staying in love. Relationships, for them, are the porcupine's dilemma. With each new lover, the rapprochement crisis is played out once again.

Upon meeting a new lover, the borderline experiences an intense need for something that has been withheld or denied her. She cannot get enough of love or sex. She clings. Without this person, she fears she will be helpless. For at least a brief period, she will idealize him as the answer to all her prayers, while, as we saw in Angela's case, she will be so involved with projecting her own desires onto this person that she will not accept him for what he is.

Margaret S. Mahler observed: "The birth of the child as an individual comes about when, in response to his mother's selective response to his cuing, the child gradually alters his behavior." But the borderline was never able to achieve such individuation. Through her identification with other people, she can relate to bits and pieces of herself, just as she can accurately perceive bits and pieces of the other person. She first forms an inaccurate impression of her lover's wants and needs, then applies those assumptions in her attempt to behave accordingly, and thus make herself loved and needed. Edward R. Shapiro insists these do not remain harmless projections, since "an unconscious attempt is made to develop a relationship with the other and to involve him as a collusive partner in conforming to the way in which he is perceived." In many cases, the partner is more than willing to perceive himself in this flattering light.

I recall, when I was in kindergarten and first grade, there was a boy named Kevin in our neighborhood. He was a year or two younger than myself, and everyone used to think he was brilliant. When he was 3 years old, my mother would talk about how she'd run into Kevin and his mother in the supermarket, and Kevin would say, "Good afternoon, Mrs. Price, how are you today?" By the time Kevin was in second grade, it was discovered that he was severely brain damaged. He overhead adult conversations, and was able to mimic them precisely, but he never developed the ability to think for himself. If he had no one to imitate, he was lost.

The borderline's emotional development could be described in similar terms: she has an extremely strong ability to mimic the emotions of a person she is close with, but little ability to formulate anything besides the most primitive emotions of her own accord. This power to mimic, and actually perceive herself as feeling, is why she continues to attach herself to another person. It is also why, as long as she is involved in a satisfactory relationship, other people will perceive her as extremely sensitive and capable.

GAINING CONTROL

We must recall that there are always two sides to the rapprochement crisis—the wish to be completely swept up by the other person, and the intense fear of engulfment. The borderline's original needs contain within them an inherent fear of the needed person. Other people might be quick to recognize the borderline's demands for an exclusive relationship with her lover, and also quickly spot how dependent she is on him, but she will herself refuse to acknowledge either her jealousy or her dependency. She will instead see him as all but helpless without her, as desperately needing her love.

Given the above relationship, based not on two people but on one person's projections onto the other, there is bound to be trouble. Since at this point the borderline, like the infant, is unable to make a distinction between herself and the other person, she will notice that the relationship is experiencing difficulties, but view those difficulties as coming from outside herself. And the minute trouble begins, she is unable to recall any good qualities about the person who frustrates her.

Nearly every person with borderline personality disorder experiences herself as the "helpless victim," not only in her history of stormy relationships, but in her childhood relation to her parents, and particularly her mother. When she was a child, she was unable to gain control over the situation. In her later relationships, she will never again permit herself to feel so powerless. Her ability to see herself as "desperately needed" while she ignores her own needs permits her to become manipulative in her attempts for control. The relationship is closer to the masochistic master-slave relationship than it is to any real love. Master and slave will, however, keep changing positions.

When she senses her relationship to be supportive, her depressive nature is activated. She becomes complacent and clings to her lover, constantly wanting greater closeness, but unable to become the instigator of any event from which they might receive mutual enjoyment. Her hold on reality, including the failures in past relationships, is at this point fairly intact, and often contributes to her passivity. At the same time, she fears becoming too dependent, and often projects her fear and hostility onto her lover. Just as he was responsive to some of her earlier projections, he will often unconsciously find himself equally responsive to this projected hostility, and thus becomes angry and controlling.

The more the borderline fears becoming controlled, the more manipulative her actions will become. As discussed in Chapter Two, these actions begin with minor outbursts of sarcasm, irritability, impatience, or bitterness. As her anxiety that she is in danger of losing this needed person increases, her measures to assert control become more drastic, culminating in extreme anger, threats of suicide, or actual self-mutilation. The extent of her aggressiveness is held in check by the very real presence of the other person, and the subconscious understanding of his value. The moment the relationship is actually perceived to end, the borderline impulsively resorts to drastic measures to escape from her own "emptiness" and create a new support network—whether human, vegetable, or institutional.

Clearly, the strain of a personal relationship places an enormous stress upon the borderline person. In the next chapter, I will describe why many borderlines turn to substance abuse and other self-destructive acts in a vain attempt to resolve the conflicts raging within themselves.

CHAPTER 5

The Illusion of Relief

Carol, age 45 and the mother of three children, keeps one chair in her living room covered with a blanket. Whenever the tension inside her becomes unbearable, she takes a butcher knife, removes the blanket, and slashes the back of that chair, over and over, until she feels better. Someday, she knows, this might not be enough to quiet all her anxieties. She's just hoping the children will be grown and away from home by then.

Sheila works as a waitress and makes decent money, but even so she's overextended on two credit cards. She had a fight with her boyfriend Thursday night. On Saturday she went shopping and spent over $1000 on new clothes—that's the third shopping spree she's gone on in the past year. "I'm entitled," she tells herself. "If guys won't buy me things then I'll buy them myself. I have a right to nice clothes, too." So she'll work extra hours for a few weeks to get more money. She'll eat only at the restaurant, and save on food. She'll manage somehow—she always did before.

Ricky, 14 years old, was brought to my office by his parents in 1983. The month before, they'd gotten a $300 phone bill; that month it was $350. Ricky would stay up half the night calling disc jockeys in Chicago, Boston, New York, and San Francisco, just to have someone to talk to. He didn't dare call the local radio station, he explained, or else the kids in school would be all over him. After the first month, he promised his parents he'd stop, but he just wasn't able to.

The three people cited above all have one thing in common: most of the people who know them think of them as extremely competent and capable. Carol has been active with the local PTA and is usually available to chauffeur her own children as well as the neighbors' to various functions. Sheila seldom misses a day of work and is willing to work overtime without any complaints; regular customers always ask to sit in her section. Ricky's grades are above average; he's a member of the marching band and the journalism club, and has never been a discipline problem at school.

So long as the borderline person is surrounded by other people, or feels herself in a structured environment, she can function with a fair degree of normalcy. There is no intended deception here—at such times she is attuned to her own capabilities. While she is experiencing this "totally good" self, she is forced to discard any memories of the "badness" she experiences in times of panic. It is, as we have seen, an extremely precarious position. This mask she is presenting to others not only covers over her feelings of inadequacy, but also makes it difficult for people to recognize how desperate and dangerous she can become.

The borderline lives from crisis to crisis. Minor, irritating events can overwhelm her. This might be best illustrated by the cliché of the harried housewife, familiar to us from any number of television comedies. She has been cooped up in the house all day with three children; one is sick, the other two haven't stopped fighting since they got home from school, a neighbor is sitting at her kitchen table chatting away, and she hasn't even had time to comb her hair. When her husband comes home an hour late and complains that his dinner's overcooked, she throws the plate in his face and bursts into tears. The husband, of course, doesn't understand what he said to set her off.

So, too, for the borderline. She has a very low tolerance for any frustration, and continually experiences herself as vulnerable, unprotected, exposed to the evils of anyone who chooses to pick on her. She handles this panic in various ways—sometimes by closing herself off, sometimes by overreacting, sometimes by escaping through the nearest exit.

"Panic," as I use the word here, implies the distress she feels at the first indications of her own aggression. She sees herself angry, about to drive away this necessary, supportive person who is the only force preventing her from falling victim to her own emptiness. She is destroying the last vestiges of goodness in herself as well as the other person, and she is convinced that the other person will retaliate. She therefore acts impulsively to make a bad situation worse.

Any action whatever will fill the space and, at least temporarily, ward off the panic. The primitive, impulsive nature of the borderline precludes any concept of time, so there is no opportunity for her to anticipate or remember—all must occur in the moment. To have stopped and thought about her actions before taking them would have required a stillness equated in her mind with the same emptiness she is trying to escape.

No one path of escape is prevalent enough to be considered a preferred course of action, yet virtually all borderlines will resort to a temporary and usually hazardous means of avoiding stressful situations. Fantasies and speech can sometimes take the place of more destructive acting-out, but the borderline's attempts to sidestep panic will frequently include drug or alcohol abuse, sexual promiscuity and deviancy, wild shopping sprees, reckless driving, kleptomania, binge eating and purging, self-mutilation, suicide threats or attempts, and other such behaviors.

I should hasten to point out, before we go any further, that the borderline does not view such actions as self-destructive or degrading. All she understands is that they have separated her from the stressful situation, prevented the "badness" from taking hold of her. At least for the time being, they have made her feel better.

John G. Gunderson has pointed out that "borderline patients are generally quite aware of social conventions—even in defiance of them." And once she has overcome the need for such acting-out behaviors, it is impossible for her to reconcile the "totally bad" self that performed those acts with the "totally good" self she fears she can never become. Unless there is some break in the cycle, it could continue this way forever. Fortunately, there is usually a climax—whether it is a serious suicide attempt or losing one's license for drunk driving, many borderlines eventually get to the point where their cries for help are heard.

ALCOHOLISM

When we realize the readiness with which liquor has become an accepted social tool in both work-related and familial situations, it should hardly surprise us that alcohol provides one of the easiest and most prominent escape hatches for borderlines. The reasons borderlines use alcohol are no different from the reasons the rest of us drink: upon entrance into new social situations, we drink as a means of lowering some of our inhibitions, dropping our defenses, and hopefully making new friends; when the friends do not materialize, or the pressures become too much, we are tempted to just continue drinking until we become oblivious to everything else.

The borderline person is trying desperately to fit in with society's conventions and to relate to other people in social situations that might lead to the intense personal relationship she desires. Before oblivion sets in, the alcohol serves to numb her panic. It is in this intoxicated state, and under the assumption that she can now gain control over some new object or person, that she frequently becomes aggressive or promiscuous.

While she is in her twenties, alcohol abuse is often a periodic act for the person with borderline personality disorder. It is an impulsive action she resorts to at times when there is no other supportive object in her environment, and will usually subside when such a support network is reinstated. But after years of moving from relationship to relationship, and feeling herself incapable of sustaining anything for very long, the borderline might well turn to alcohol as her primary source of comfort. It is estimated that as many as 30 percent of female alcoholics would meet the other diagnostic criteria for borderline personality disorder.

DRUG ABUSE

Borderline personality disorder has been almost unique to the past three decades—the same period that produced the hippies and the flower children—decades during which the use of illegal drugs has played the role of social equalizer among our youth in much the manner that alcohol served previous generations. To this day, drug abuse is one of the most common forms of "acting-out" among borderline adolescents. Many impulsively experiment with various drugs both as adjunct to relating and as an escape from relationships. The adolescent who, whether borderline or not, does not see the use of drugs as either addictive or self-degrading has become a pitiful cliché in our society. To complicate matters further, the borderline's unstable image of herself makes her especially susceptible to psychotic episodes under the influence of hallucinogens such as mescaline or LSD, and to episodes of either paranoia or paranoid psychosis under the influence of marijuana.

A person cannot always turn to drugs for brief periods when a relationship is perceived to be in jeopardy, and then discard them once she receives validation from other sources. Once you become addicted, deeper problems set in. In this case, drug addiction itself adds to the problems of finding a stable, supportive relationship. Again, we see here the childlike behavior of the borderline person who will not (and in many cases *cannot*) assume responsibility for an adult life.

PROMISCUITY

I first met Cindi when she was referred to me for treatment by a friend who runs an employment agency. Extremely attractive and capable, with a Master's degree in Journalism, Cindi was 29 years old and had recently been fired from her job as an account executive with a large advertising agency. This was the third job she'd been fired from in the past four years, this time for "unacceptable associations with clients and potential clients." Previous employers had phrased it differently, but all the statements added up to the fact that men found Cindi attractive, Cindi found men attractive, and becoming sexually involved was the only way she knew of relating to them—whether they were clients or co-workers.

"I swore this time I wouldn't let it happen," Cindi told me. "And I was good, I was much better. I only got involved with one guy from the office, and he wasn't married, something really could have happened between us. But that didn't work out, and I was meeting with clients, there was no one else around, it didn't seem as if we'd be hurting anyone. I guess it just isn't in me to be cold to men. But it's more than that. If I wake up on a morning when I haven't spent the night with someone, I feel so bored, it's almost as if I don't exist. What's wrong with me?"

I didn't have to look very far to know what was "wrong" with Cindi—I see patients like her several times a day. Cindi was one of the luckier ones. She'd moved from job to job, but she thought enough of herself to seek out fairly high-level employment. The office environment, with cubbyholes giving an illusion of privacy while managers watched every movement, provided enough structure so that once she'd made up her mind to succeed this time, Cindi was able to function fairly well within it. Away from the office, at meetings with clients, she was left to her own devices, and this is where she fell apart.

Most of Cindi's "affairs" were one-night stands. She made sure that all the men took precautions against disease. But now, especially since she was out of a job again, she was becoming frightened that she'd get to the point where she no longer cared, and wanted help before it went too far. As Cindi put it, "I don't trust myself."

Little wonder, considering her earlier statement about feeling bored and almost nonexistent on those mornings when she woke up alone. Confused and uncertain about her inner identity, she is able to make herself available in only a superficial, physical manner. Subconsciously aware of her need to run away from any stressful, intense relationship, she uses her physical body as its own barrier—this far and no farther, or watch out, I'm warning you.

Sexual promiscuity, extremely common among borderlines, is one more way of filling up the emptiness. Even when a woman like Cindi begins to see the self-destructive results of her actions, she has no concept of their self-degrading nature. Her need is greater than just using the radio or television to give off the soothing sounds of voices; she sees herself in a desperate search for some idealized person who doesn't exist. More important, he can't exist. Cindi, like most other borderlines, would be so threatened by his presence that she'd either drive him away or run away herself.

As we will see in Chapter Eleven, one of the main goals in

psychiatric therapy with borderline patients is to bring them to the point where they can unite the "good" and "bad" in themselves and other people. Only once they achieve such a position will they be able to enter into a sustained and mutually rewarding relationship. In the meantime, as the old song goes, if you can't be with the one you love, love the one you're with—a song that a borderline person can identify with.

SEXUAL DEVIANCE

"I just wish I could decide what I want," Brian told me the first time I saw him. "I can go to a party with a woman and go home with a man. Or I think I'll make things simpler and go with a man to begin with, then find myself getting interested in all the women. I end up alienating everyone. And I'm still not satisfied."

The DSM-III-R diagnostic criteria cite "marked and persistent identity disturbance" as a symptom in borderline personality disorder, and lists "self-image" and "sexual orientation" as two of its possible manifestations. Certainly borderlines frequently display a preoccupation with sex, often aided by the simultaneous use of alcohol and drugs. A wide variety of sexual desires, including desires to perform perverse acts, have been discovered in borderline persons who during their calmer periods view such actions as one more confirmation of how "totally bad" they are.

In 1986, pilot studies were conducted with borderline patients at McClean Hospital in Belmont, Massachusetts, and the Western Psychiatric Institute in Pittsburgh. Between 50 and 60 percent of the males participating in these studies were also discovered to be homosexual (ten times higher than the figures Kinsey gives for male homosexuality among the general population). Eleven percent of the women proved to be homosexual (a figure six times greater than that given by Kinsey for female homosexuality among the general population).

The authors take care to note, however, that the combination of homosexuality and borderline personality disorder might greatly increase the likelihood of a person seeking professional help, so the figures in their study might not be as reflective of the general population as they at first appear. They also report that "the presence of homosexuality in patients of either sex was not associated with a significantly higher number or greater severity of borderline symptoms."

In a similar study of twenty men and thirty women in the same age group (18 to 37 years), meeting the criteria for major depression but not for borderline personality disorder, only one man and none of the women met criteria for homosexuality. The authors also suggest: "Several lines of evidence suggest that the observed higher rate of homosexuality among men with borderline personality disorder, which predominantly affects women, may be analogous to the reported increased rate of homosexuality among women with sociopathy, which predominantly affects men."

EATING DISORDERS

Listen to one 16-year-old borderline patient:
"I don't really know why I stopped eating. I just sort of did it—and at the time it seemed the thing to do. I certainly didn't want to get fat and lazy like my sister. Then at first I was waiting for my parents to notice how much weight I was losing, but they didn't seem to care enough to look that closely. And if they don't care, I mean, why bother?"

In recent years, eating disorders such as anorexia nervosa and bulimia have sometimes been found to be an early indication of borderline personality disorder. As in the case above, this can be used as a form of manipulation, a desperate act to get another person to care—another example of darting-away behavior. Like other borderline symptoms, anorexia frequently coincides with adolescence. Once again, the child has entered into a stage of development where she is expected to venture farther away from her mother, and once again her fears of being either engulfed in her mother's love or left to the mercies of an unstable self have made it impossible for her to function. By stubbornly refusing to eat, and often finding it impossible to eat, the patient is expressing her fear of growing apart—the "fatness" can be seen as a metaphor for femininity or adult sexuality.

Bulimia, a related diagnosis sometimes found concurrently with anorexia nervosa, involves repetitive binges of overeating followed by self-induced vomiting and purging. In this instance, the concept of "filling" the emptiness can be taken almost literally—the borderline first overeats, then regrets her actions and forces her body to reject the food. Bulimia is most easily linked to the borderline diagnosis by its impulsive, acting-out nature, and its illusion of control. While there are often physical as well as psychological causes for such symptoms, one could make similar statements regarding drug or alcohol abuse.

ADOLESCENT SELF-DESTRUCTION CONTINUED: A WORLD OF ITS OWN

Lynn had been caught cheating on two previous history tests, and was warned that if it happened again she would be suspended from school. Despite the warnings, Lynn sat in the classroom during the last test and continually referred to a notepad on her lap. It was discovered that the notepad contained only nonsense words, but that didn't matter. The class had been told that no papers other than the tests were permitted in the classroom. Lynn had disobeyed this, and was suspended.

Taking risks is an expected, and needed, facet of adolescence. I will always recall the scene in the movie *Rebel Without a Cause*, in which the boys get their kicks by driving junk cars toward the cliff—whoever jumps first is chicken. Or there is a scene in the movie, *Stand By Me* in which the boys kneel on the railroad tracks until they hear the train's vibrations as close as they dare.

But here a distinction must be made between the normal adolescent who is testing the limits society will tolerate in order to gain a better sense of self and the borderline adolescent who is using such acts to avoid assuming responsibility. Thus Bobby, a normal adolescent, might drive his car at eighty miles an hour so that he can feel free and in control of the vehicle, while David, a borderline adolescent, drives at eighty miles an hour because he feels as if he has nothing to lose or because the speed takes away his feeling of emptiness. David not only does not have control over the vehicle (or his life), he does not *want* control. On the surface, both behaviors might appear the same, but the normal adolescent will grow out of them, while the borderline will continue to find new ways to self-destruct.

In 1979, before borderline personality disorder was an officially recognized diagnosis, Dr. Daniel Offer and his associates studied 55 juvenile delinquents and defined four clinical types: the impulsive, the narcissistic, the depressed borderline, and the empty borderline. He further described the two borderline conditions as follows: "The depressed borderline is often well liked, shows initiative in school, has considerable guilt and depression, and acts out mainly to relieve this depression. The empty borderline is extremely passive, often not liked, and emotionally depleted. For these delinquents, acting out behavior is in the service of warding off psychotic disintegration or fragmentation and reducing intense inner emptiness."

Borderline adolescents are especially creative at self-destruction. In his many articles on adolescent borderlines, James F. Masterson talks about how they would come into his office with a proud grin on their faces about their latest act, sort of like a sculpture that they were bringing in to show the therapist.

SUICIDE AS A FORM OF MANIPULATION

Suicide is the borderline person's most effective manipulative tool. The image of Alex, the character Glenn Close plays in *Fatal Attraction*, stays in my mind as I write this. Dan (Michael Douglas) has spent Saturday night and part of Sunday with her—less than twenty-four hours. He gets out of bed and begins dressing to go home, while she screams at him not to leave. He goes in the bathroom to wash up and emerges to find she has slit her wrists. Dan does what any considerate human being would do: he bandages her wrists and spends another night with her. Alex didn't really cause herself that much pain, and she got what she wanted. The manipulation worked.

As discussed in Chapter Four, Alex's actions throughout the first half of *Fatal Attraction* are typically those of the borderline person. According to a *People* magazine article, in the film's original ending Alex slit her throat to the music of *Madama Butterfly*. She used a knife that contained Dan's fingerprints, thus harming both herself and the lover who abandoned her. Pilot audiences, however, refused to accept that ending.

As we will see, such manipulative self-destruction would have been far more typical of borderline behavior than the actions that were substituted in the ending of *Fatal Attraction* as it was finally released. While borderlines have been known to set the homes or offices of their lovers or their therapists on fire, tear up the wardrobes of a former lover, make threatening phone calls, or smash the windows of a hospital whose support they pleaded for only a few hours before, it is far more likely that they will turn their most extreme anger against themselves. After all, Angela's knife only cut herself, not me.

To the great distress of their family and friends, borderline patients threaten and attempt suicide more frequently than the schizophrenic or depressed patients with whom most of us are more familiar. In actual point of fact, however, only 8 to 10 percent of people with borderline personality disorder actually commit suicide, a relatively small number when placed alongside the number of people who threaten suicide or make manipulative suicide attempts. Even so, we would be denying our own humanity if we pretended not to respond to these attempts with the utmost concern.

By calling such threats "manipulative," I imply that the borderline uses them not with the intention of actually killing herself, but as a device to get other people to comply with her desires. Such attempts will be made at a time when other people can be expected to find out about it and respond before it is too late. In *Fatal Attraction*, Alex slits her wrists before Dan leaves the apartment, then goes over to hug him to be certain he'll notice the blood.

"I called from the office to say I'd be working late," the single mother of Janet, a hospitalized borderline adolescent who had just entered treatment, told me. "I asked her to heat up dinner for the younger kids, but she started screaming at me about not caring whether she lived or died, so finally I said okay, I'd finish the letters I was typing and come home. What was the point of her swallowing all those pills? She knew I'd find her before they could take effect."

That was the point precisely. At that moment, Janet didn't know of any other way to convince her mother and the rest of the world of how desperate she was feeling. She'd gone into a tantrum on the phone, and her mother had agreed to come home, but even in her mother's retelling of the incident, she had conveyed her disgust and anger with such childish behavior. So Janet had swallowed a bottle of aspirin that was in the medicine cabinet.

When she was a little girl, Janet's mother told me, Janet used to beat her head against the wall in an attempt to get her way. Her mother generally ignored her behavior, but on two occasions when it looked like physical damage might result, she tied her to a chair. After these attacks subsided, Janet was sent to her room and not permitted out until she was ready to apologize.

Janet's mother loved her very much, but she also saw no reason why she should put up with such behavior. And for a brief period during her early adolescence, such behavior stopped. Like the younger children in the family, Janet learned to do what she was told without too much protest, while her mother was able to ignore the fact that Janet was more vulnerable than her other children. When the pressures finally became too much, a manipulative suicide attempt was the only way Janet could think of to make certain her mother didn't just write her desperation off as childish and dismiss it once again.

Such behavior is not limited to adolescents. Every day hospitals admit men and women of all ages under similar circumstances—women who swallowed pills an hour before their husbands were due home from work or their children were due home from school, men and women who overdosed and then panicked five minutes later and called a friend to get them help, women who locked the bathroom door and slit their wrists when they were certain someone else would need the bathroom soon.

Erica, another patient who was referred to me, went into the kitchen to get the dessert for a dinner party. She closed the kitchen door silently behind her and stuck her head in the oven. Her friends found her a few minutes later, already passed out. When I inquired as to the reason, Erica told me that Matt, her boyfriend, had been flirting with one of the women at the party. This time, Erica's act was prompted by her rage at her boyfriend. Six months before, after another dinner party, she had slit her wrists in an effort to punish herself because she was a terrible cook and no one at the party had praised the food as much as she'd been expecting.

"One of these times you're going to go too far," Erica's sister screamed at her while she was in the hospital. "One of these times no one's going to find you!"

It's easy to see why manipulative suicide attempts are seldom singular in nature: the manipulation worked once, so it's bound to work again. Every time some borderline persons feel the least bit in danger of being abandoned, they threaten suicide, and if the threat does not immediately provoke a response, they slash their wrists or swallow a few pills. Since they have no real concept of their own self-destructiveness, they're betting that they won't take it too far. Of course, I have seen many "miscalculations" that ended in disaster.

Which of us has never crossed a street against the light? We've looked, there's no car in sight, we're betting that we'll be safely across before that bus two blocks down gets here. We know we're tempting fate a bit, but that's part of everyday life. For the borderline, manipulative suicide is a part of everyday life. It is not the easiest escape route; it has become the *only* escape route.

WHEN MANIPULATION STOPS

"Please don't leave me alone, I'm frightened," the borderline woman screams as her lover is leaving for the tenth time that month. Yes, there is a form of manipulation here; she would do or say anything to keep him from leaving. But there is also a real fear that should not be underestimated. Her whole life history tells her that if the pain gets too much to bear, she'll be forced to harm herself.

All the self-destructive acts we have examined so far have been intended either to manipulate and control some person the borderline felt might be on the verge of abandoning her, or as part of a desperate, futile search for some new sustaining relationship. As we saw in Chapter Two, so long as the borderline's relation to a supportive person remains intact, serious self-destructive behavior does not occur. When the threat of loss becomes apparent to the borderline, manipulative acts of increasing seriousness will occur, sometimes culminating in threats of suicide or mild suicide attempts. No matter how destructive these acts might appear to other people, the borderline sees them as protecting herself from suffering the greater harm that would result from actual abandonment.

But there are other times when the borderline attempts to kill herself, times when she doesn't expect—moreover doesn't want—to be saved. At such times her feelings of "badness" are so deep that she is convinced she doesn't deserve to live. Left to her own devices, the emptiness can become unbearable. One more drink or going on a shopping spree or finding a new partner to sleep with tonight simply isn't sufficient. She feels, literally, as if she's popping out of her skin, and the only relief in sight is to open the skin so that she won't feel so constrained.

At moments like this, a woman such as Erica is likely to slit her wrists or burn herself. She gives a sigh of relief as she watches the blood pour out or the skin begin to blister. She is delighted to see the "badness" escaping her, maybe for good this time; maybe this time she'll remain cleansed. In the beginning the feeling of relief from tension is so strong that it's as if she's under anaesthesia. Later, when the pain begins, it's a good feeling—if she can experience pain, then she must not be completely "bad" or "empty." There are a number of borderlines for whom this is the most efficient method of relieving tension, and such self-mutilation is an immediate response to pressure.

"I told George I'd never hurt anyone, and I couldn't understand why he felt so threatened that he had to cut my wrists like that," another new patient, Jamie, told me the first time I saw her. "I honestly didn't realize George had gone home, that's how out of it I was. I don't understand what happened to me."

It wasn't the first time I'd seen a borderline patient whose suicide attempt had been accompanied by a brief psychotic episode in which the absent person played a major role. Sometimes, as in Jamie's case, the patient fantasizes that this absent person is actually performing the destructive act, while the borderline continues seeing herself as "good" and undeserving of such destruction. At other times, the borderline patient fantasizes that this absent person is present while she is harming herself and the other person is punished by her actions. Either way, she is not left alone to face herself.

CHAPTER 6

Getting Help

One of my fondest memories was, years ago, going to see a close friend in the hospital just after she'd given birth to her first child. Before going into her room, I stopped to look in the nursery. My friend's baby, Andrew, was the only infant crying, just as her husband, Bob, was going in to hold him. Through the window, I could see Bob's lips moving, and I watched as Andrew calmed down. Afterward, as we walked down the corridor, Bob, a former blues pianist, told me he wasn't quite sure what he should have done with a crying infant, but—figuring the baby had a lot to cry about—he started to sing a blues ballad. Andrew didn't seem to care that his father wasn't singing a lullaby; he only knew he was being held and soothed.

Like my friend's baby, the majority of people with borderline personality disorder who begin therapy don't precisely understand why. It doesn't necessarily ring a bell with them that they have a specific problem that needs attention; there's more of a vague sense that something's wrong. For many of these people, their impatience and demandingness had begun to create problems at work or in relationships, problems that may have led them into therapy.

I've had borderline patients come in complaining of panic attacks; who were abusing alcohol and been arrested for DWI or whatever; who had gotten into serious financial difficulty by spending all their money. Very often a borderline patient has recently split up with someone she cared about and can't seem to shake the depression. For many borderlines, why they seek treatment is not as important as entering into treatment. For these patients, the chief complaint or problem that caused them to seek help to begin with is a symptom of something much larger. Part of the therapist's job in the first few sessions will be a process of gathering information until the underlying issues become clear to the therapist.

THE FREEDOM TO MOVE

"When Karen called to say she was dropping out of therapy two months ago, that was the last straw. This was the third doctor she'd seen in the past seven years, and every time it seemed as if she was coping better, she would quit therapy and then quickly get worse. 'Go ahead,' I told her, 'drop out if you want to, but don't expect me to pay for another shrink.' I'd really had it. But I don't know, doctor, I really can't give up on her. Maybe you can help her."

—FATHER OF A 25-YEAR-OLD BORDERLINE PATIENT

Borderline persons often enter into therapy with the same *magical expectations* with which they approach other relationships. The new patient views the therapist as her savior, an all-powerful individual who is going to absorb all her pains and problems and transform her into a happy, healthy person, usually without any involvement or action on her own part. It's not surprising then, that many borderlines, having failed to find their savior, disappointedly drop out of therapy. Many new patients of mine complain that their previous experiences with therapy only made them feel worse.

But becoming disillusioned with a therapist and discontinuing treatment is not necessarily an indication that they gained little from the experience. If nothing else, the obstacles patients seemed on the verge of overcoming with one therapist might well prepare them to begin treatment again with another doctor. And this time, they should be slightly better able to cope with the frustrations that always emerge when one enters a relationship, even a therapeutic one. Those patients who repeatedly drop out of therapy for brief periods, only to pick it up again with another therapist, are following a typical borderline pattern of calling out for help, then moving from relationship to relationship as each idealized person proves incapable of meeting their expectations. While the family of such a patient might wish for more sustained treatment, it's important not to jump to hasty conclusions. Such conclusions, in effect, mirror and thus reinforce the borderline person's own impulsive reactions.

There are many reasons for borderlines moving from therapist to therapist, not the least of which is the borderline's inability to hold on to a particular job. I have had some patients who, early in the course of therapy, lost their jobs and either their medical insurance or their ability to pay for psychiatric care, and therefore had to drop out of therapy. Far more frequently, however, patients drop out of therapy because either the therapist and the patient are poorly matched to begin with, or because there had been no clear understanding of what could be expected from the therapeutic involvement.

FINDING THE RIGHT THERAPIST

When a mother decides to give her 6-year-old daughter piano lessons, she does not necessarily send her to the famous music teacher lecturing at the local university. She understands, without thinking about the matter too closely, that such a magnificent teacher might not have the skills and patience necessary to work with a very young, beginning student. In a similar manner, even some of the best therapists might not have the proper skills and personalities to work with borderline patients.

Treating borderlines effectively is not easy—it takes a rather thick-skinned, patient, and sensitive therapist to see past the verbal onslaughts and mercurial tempers of borderlines to appreciate their good side. In addition, the desperate fanaticism with which a borderline may approach therapy may not appeal to every therapist. As Edward R. Shapiro pointed out: "Many therapists who have devoted their lives to healing are concerned at some level about their capacity to hurt, which borderline patients unconsciously sense." And, I might add, once this is sensed by the borderline patient, it can be used as a means of manipulating the therapist.

The therapist who works with borderline patients must be sensitive to his own experiences of separation and willing to share some of those experiences with the patients as therapy progresses. In a sense, he identifies with what the patient is experiencing, yet at the same time he does not share the patient's view of the separation as needless and intolerable. The therapist must also feel comfortable with his own aggression, so that he does not merely react to the patient's unavoidable anger. Many borderline patients have never before had the experience of venting their anger without driving away the person they cared about. The very fact that the therapist is able to tolerate their anger without retaliating sets the stage for the necessary risks both the patient and the therapist will have to take as the treatment continues.

If the process of finding the right therapist, then sticking with the treatment at least long enough to effect some important changes, is ever going to flow smoothly, it might be worth spending a little time here looking at what sorts of psychiatric treatment are available to the borderline person. It should be pointed out that many of the leading psychiatric theorists have written about treating borderline personality disorder in recent years, each advocating a specific technique. The discrepancies between these various techniques seem much more distinct on paper than they do when it comes to treating individual patients. Most good therapists end up using a combination of various methods at different stages in the treatment.

SUPPORTIVE PSYCHOTHERAPY

In supportive psychotherapy, the main emphasis is on helping the patient to feel better and function better within an environment that she has no capacity to change. It is also the therapy of choice for many patients who don't have the financial resources necessary to enter into more intensive treatment. Such patients often find themselves going to community mental health centers, where the staff changes before a structured therapeutic relationship can be established.

In the effort to help, the supportive psychotherapist might reassure, advise, and attempt to educate or reeducate the patient. And in response to supportive psychotherapy, most borderline patients *can* and *do* show a marked improvement in a relatively quick period of time. Their ability to function in social situations becomes more manageable; they have a comfortable environment in which to discuss some of their frustrations.

Even in cases where the patient is acting merely to gain the therapist's approval, such patients frequently find themselves better able to organize their lives and assume responsibilities. Self-destructive acts become less frequent, and supportive psychotherapy can be extremely useful as a crisis intervention. At best, supportive psychotherapy focuses on the practical issues of living in a chaotic, highly pressured world. It attempts to maintain the status quo of an individual on a day-to-day basis, without probing emotional conflicts too deeply. Its long-term goals, therefore, are limited.

I personally see supportive psychotherapy as taking a rather pessimistic view of the capabilities of the borderline patient. Intensive, exploratory, psychoanalytically oriented psychotherapy takes a much more optimistic approach as to what can be accomplished—and if you're not optimistic about a borderline patient's ability to restructure what is essentially a personality defect, then you really shouldn't be working with her. Borderlines have suffered enough already. For most of them, the past was extremely frustrating, and they're not capable of envisioning a future that will be any better. The therapist's conviction that each patient is capable of working through past failures and overcoming present and future failures is essential if the patient is going to be able to withstand the additional pressures that arise as she looks closely at herself. If the therapist is not convinced of the patient's inner resources, her ability to achieve love and a mature relationship, then perhaps there is no reason to subject her to further turmoil. But I *must* add that I've met very few borderline patients about whom I was this pessimistic.

Otto F. Kernberg refers to supportive therapy as pulling out the handkerchiefs. Most borderline patients will need more support, especially at the beginning of treatment, than other patients. They're setting up a relationship with a therapist whom they'll see two or three hours a week, and their fear of abandonment is going to be at its height. Any good therapist has to be available for phone calls and extra appointments from time to time. A soothing environment helps the borderline patient through the first few months of treatment; then aspects of that soothing continue through the length of the treatment. To return to Kernberg's metaphor: I carry a handkerchief at all times, and I'm perfectly willing to pull it out occasionally working with patients, but at the same time I'm working on confronting and interpreting the larger issues that arise during treatment.

INTENSIVE, EXPLORATORY THERAPY

Psychoanalyis in the classical, Freudian approach means lying down on the couch and not facing the therapist. The therapist has little or no verbal involvement in the therapy. That's a relatively unstructured hour for the patient, and most therapists discover it's not the best way to treat borderlines. It's also next to impossible—I can't see how even the strictest Freudians could remain cold and unresponsive to the borderline patient in the midst of a panic or anxiety attack.

Intensive psychotherapy combines the above with a more interactive approach; the therapist sets limits and contributes verbally at times within the psychoanalytic structure. Using transference and confrontational techniques, the therapist attempts to restructure the ways in which the patient interprets reality. There is an attempt to uncover and explore the aspects of the past that the patient is attempting to repress and to confront directly how the past has affected her ability to function in the present. From my point of view, most borderlines are capable of responding to this sort of therapy—they have proved, in fact, distinctly more responsive than patients with schizoid or paranoid disorders.

On a practical level, the patient, at least in the beginning, must be capable of arranging therapy appointments at least twice, and preferably three times, per week. If deeper issues are going to be worked through, it will take time and effort on the part of both the therapist and the patient. And borderline patients, in particular, are susceptible to running away from confrontational situations. Seeing a patient once a week, it is almost impossible to provide enough support and structure to get them past such periodic regressions.

HOW SUPPORTIVE IS THE SUPPORT?

I'm aware of some agencies who treat borderlines without establishing a treatment structure or setting up parameters. If the patient misses an appointment the counselors don't say anything about it; if the patient is twenty minutes late, it's no big deal, come whenever you can. That very lack of limits could be seen as supportive to the patient, but it actually *impedes* treatment. A borderline patient needs a structured setting with appointments, times, and payments. Actually these parameters will be some of the issues that will lead to meaningful confrontations.

When you confront borderline patients, you're liable to get an incredible amount of anger, and that can be frightening to a therapist sitting in a small room with someone who looks like they're going to explode. When you're working with a borderline patient sometimes it's easier, under the guise of being supportive, to not stand by the usual therapeutic limitations.

I wrote earlier that borderline patients need quite a bit of support, especially during the first stages of treatment. But even within this situation, which some therapists refer to as a "holding environment," there can be some parameters established. If I have a borderline patient whom I see on Mondays and Thursdays, but who calls me every day, I might say, "Listen, I can't talk to you now, but I'm going to reserve Tuesday at 3:15—you can call me then and tell me what's going on, what kinds of problems have arisen. Whenever possible, why don't you save up some of the things that appear so urgent in the moment, and call me at those times?"

WHO'S RESPONSIBLE HERE?

The therapist is not the patient's mother. Much as the borderline patient would like to be taken care of, it must be made clear that the therapist will not attempt to do for the patient what she cannot or will not do for herself. If the therapeutic relationship stands any chance of succeeding, the patient must be willing to understand her own contribution to the process and be willing to take at least partial responsibility for her impulsive actions and their subsequent effects.

The borderline uses primitive forms of projection to protect herself from her own aggression, then denies its existence within her "good" self. Particularly when a patient is involved in self-destructive behavior, the therapist's first task is to control such behaviors by repeatedly pointing out their potential harm—not only to the patient's physical health, but to her ability to function on a day-to-day basis, and to the chances of making progress in the therapy. "If you're too drunk to work and call in sick again, your boss warned you he'll start looking for a replacement," I might tell a fairly new patient. Gradually, at the therapist's prompting, the patient begins to think before she acts.

If a therapist is providing supportive therapy, he might well help the borderline patient make decisions. While that's always a temptation, the goal of intensive, exploratory therapy is simply to raise questions in the patient's mind regarding her behavior. Because such impulsive actions were defensive to begin with, we can see why the patient forced to question her behavior will necessarily become more frustrated. She expected easy answers. She expected to be taken care of. The therapist reiterates that no one will gain if he merely provides for her. The patient may show rage and accuse the therapist of not caring. Here again, the fact that he is not frightened off by her aggressive behavior speaks much louder than words.

Early in the treatment, the therapist shares with the patient his understanding that therapy will not necessarily progress smoothly, that there might be long periods when she will leave the office more depressed or anxious than when she came in. As treatment progresses, he continually rephrases this concept in different ways. Once the patient accepts this, she also assumes responsibility for any acting-out behaviors such anxiety spurs. These brief regressions are to be expected with borderline patients; the reasons for them, and the forms they often take, will be discussed further in Chapter Nine.

It is only after this initial defensive behavior has broken down, and is to an extent controllable, that the real therapeutic work can begin. Once patient and therapist have entered jointly into intensive exploratory therapy, two processes will stand out as important indicators of the process: transference and interpretation.

TRANSFERENCE

Transference—the patient's ability to let the analyst take the place of the parent, acting and feeling toward him the way she did (or wishes she could) toward her parents—is seldom a stumbling block in establishing a therapeutic relationship with borderlines. The borderline approaches therapy all too desirous of such a relationship. This might be better understood if we recall my assertion in the Introduction that "there is no such thing as a borderline person who is not receiving help—if he or she does not seek out a professional, help is gained through the nurturance of other people." A brief look at the borderline's history of tumultuous relationships reveals the way in which this very need for a transference figure has driven away the people she wanted most. As I pointed out above, one of the first revelations to the borderline in treatment is that here, finally, is a person who can safely withstand her aggression.

There is both a positive and a negative aspect to this transference process with borderline patients. Just as with her other relationships, the borderline establishes a view of the therapist as all-powerful and capable of no harm. At such times, many borderline patients will attempt to "trick" him into assuming responsibility for their lives. Borderlines have proved themselves especially adept at manipulation and attempts to gain control of the therapist. And if he still does not respond, the therapist, like everyone else in the borderline's life, quickly becomes the "all bad" person who "does not deserve to live."

I think of myself as a very patient person in the long run, whatever I might be at a given moment. When I think of tolerance, I think of my capacity to sit there and work with a patient who seems very angry at me for something I have not done. I've got to be able to look behind what I hear and what I feel. I cannot do what the borderline patient does—see only a rotten person and their anger. I know there's something better there. That kind of optimism is a necessity in treating borderlines.

As I described earlier, the borderline has a poorly defined concept of "self" and "other." In her ordinary relationships, she is perfectly capable of confusing her projections of what she needs from the other person with what the other person is actually doing, saying, or feeling. This projection can happen during treatment as well. A session I recorded with Nancy, a 24-year-old borderline patient, is useful here. Nancy, who had entered therapy during an intense depression after her latest relationship dissolved, was telling me about a man she'd seen the past weekend:

"Bruce was hemming and hawing on the phone, finally he said he'd really like it if we could go out for dinner before the party, but he wouldn't get a paycheck for another two weeks, and wasn't sure he could afford it. So the choices were to either eat alone, go to a coffee shop, or go out for a nice dinner and split the bill. I told him let's go out for a nice dinner. A woman paying her own way is nothing so unusual these days. We had wine with dinner, which was fine with me, I was able to keep a pretty good hold on myself and not drink too much. And at the party I felt good, I was dressed properly for once. That's what happens when you care about yourself enough to take a little extra time dressing. The whole party was no big thing, but at least I didn't go home crying to myself that I'd blown it. Bruce didn't make any overtures to spend the night, and I didn't feel rejected. I'm proud."

As we were sitting there talking, I at first took Nancy's monologue at face value. But later I realized that it was a dialogue in which Nancy had internalized my responses. In effect, to get my approval, she was incorporating my words, my phrases, my reactions into her descriptions: "A woman paying her own way is nothing so unusual these days... That's what happens when you care about yourself enough to take a little extra time dressing... I'm proud." I should emphasize that Nancy was completely unaware she was doing this.

But there is one more important stumbling-block here. As can be seen from the above monologue, Nancy was using her projection of my approval to reinforce her actions, and was able to feel good about this new man in her life. The opposite could just as easily have occurred: a situation in which she would have projected my disapproval and absorbed what she perceived as my anger to assist her own aggressive behavior. Times when the therapist is idealized will coincide with periods of calm in other relationships. For the patient not in a supportive relationship, these periods will coincide with better contact being established in casual relationships.

The patient who feels herself being "denied" the good therapist, or is threatened by developments that have arisen in the therapeutic process, will similarly become antagonistic and overly critical of other major people in her life. Or, to reverse the situation, the patient who senses antagonism and fears abandonment in a long-term relationship might well channel all her anger and aggression toward the therapist. By examining and understanding the inflated importance of a therapist, the patient uncovers her own separation anxieties and fears of experiencing the feelings of helplessness and vulnerability that are a part of every normal relationship.

Gradually, through the process of transference, confrontation, and interpretation, the patient is brought to understand her own fear of aggression and her pattern of continually projecting it onto other people in order to protect herself. Kernberg has stated that a shift in transference patterns from those of primitive projections to the realistic ability to see the therapist as a real person with his own desires and needs are an important indicator of the patient's newfound maturity.

INTERPRETATION: THE HERE AND NOW

Remember the story about the baby and his blues-singing father that opened this chapter? Well, the same can be said regarding interpretations that the therapist makes in working with a borderline patient: they might not understand the words, but they relate to the gesture. There are several different opinions as to whether or not the borderline can understand the verbal content of what is being said, but my own feeling is that it doesn't matter. The psychiatrist is there, working with them, speaking with them, and if the words aren't yet understood, that does not diminish their soothing effect. What's important is that the process is beginning, and will continue, and if everyone takes enough time and effort, sooner or later some of its meaning will take hold.

The borderline has followed a lifelong pattern of hearing not what is said, but what she wants to hear. Her conversations with the therapist can be expected to follow the same pattern. Every time the therapist makes a comment, the patient will distort it to a greater or lesser extent. It is up to the therapist to continually clarify any misinterpretations. Little by little, her primitive defenses are replaced by mature reasoning. Once this happens, the borderline can listen to interpretations and questions without immediately distorting what is being said.

Every patient is different. I can't make a hard and fast rule and say I'm not going to make any interpretations during the first six months of treatment, or during the first year of treatment, or whatever. In general, I try not to make any interpretations during the first three or four months. And even then, the concept of "interpretation" has to be slightly altered when you're working with a borderline. Interpretation, in its strictest sense, refers to the process the therapist uses to make the patient understand the reasons behind her emotional problems and subsequent behavior.

You never make a "genetic" interpretation (relating childhood to the present) with a borderline patient. When I was first working with Nancy, for example, I couldn't say: "You're refusing to let your new boyfriend out of your sight because you're afraid. You remember how often, when you were a child, your parents weren't there for you, and you're afraid that's going to happen with everyone else you care about." A statement like that would be precisely the sort of thing that would set Nancy, or any other borderline, off on the wrong track. She'd take it as an attack, and she might come back and say "Well, that proves how rotten I am. I'm just the sort of awful person whose parents would do something like that."

For the borderline, everything, including interpretation, has to be focused on the here and now. The borderline has enough distortions about what happens in the present; there's no point in confusing things further by trying to interpret what happened in the past. I do not mean that what happened in the past is not important, only that it is more productive to focus on the present.

As we saw in Chapter Three, the formation of borderline personality disorder began with the experiences of early childhood. With the borderline, as with any other patient, the psychiatrist begins by going over the patient's family history. It's important for the *therapist* to clarify what the patient's past has been like; whether or not he shares these observations with the patient is another matter. And here I can only point out once again that the longer one works with such a patient, the better able one is to see the discrepancy between what really happened and the patient's memory of what happened. On closer look, there are seldom any monsters.

When, in one of the first sessions I had with her, Nancy joyously told me how she hadn't let her boyfriend out of her sight all weekend, I understood the relation to her childhood. But instead of referring to that, I asked her where he'd wanted to go on his own. She told me he wanted to go to the newsstand, and I questioned how far the newsstand was from her house. I asked how long it would take him to get there and back. Without much further prompting, Nancy admitted that maybe she'd been a bit silly not to have let him go out for fifteen minutes without her. I decided not to press the issue further at that time.

But again, it was important to recognize that Nancy had spent a rewarding weekend with someone she cared about, which made it that much easier for her to calmly accept the realization I was steering her toward. Had the boyfriend gone off angry when she tried to keep him at her side, she might well have been outraged by my question of how long it took to get to the newsstand and back.

I stated earlier that the borderline's therapeutic transferences are influenced by the anxiety she feels regarding other important people in her life. Her ability to make sense of interpretations is similarly reliant. Many psychiatrists judge a patient's ability to benefit from interpretation and confrontation by whether or not they have supportive people outside the therapeutic relationship, people who can help them deal with some of the anxiety the close look at their actions might have aroused.

Borderline persons are notorious for their elaborate efforts to escape confrontation. The easiest escape route, in therapy as in other life situations, is angry manipulation. Borderline patients will frequently attempt to avoid dealing with the therapist's interpretations by searching for and pointing out minute contradictions between something said today and something said several months ago. Again, it is the therapist's job not to get caught up in the anger, but to cut through the patient's defenses and draw attention back to the here and now. Only then can she focus on the immediate causes, not the effects.

When we think about subjecting most patients to psychoanalysis, we consider it a process of "making the unconscious conscious." When working with people who have borderline personality disorder, even this conception must be modified. The borderline is all too much in touch with her unconscious: she is haunted by it; she has spent the better part of her life in failed attempts to repress the aggression it has caused. When I stated that interpretation for borderlines is focused on the here and now, I hoped to imply that we are interpreting not the unconscious wishes, but the impulsive actions the borderline uses to protect herself against acknowledging those wishes. Otto F. Kernberg refers to working with borderlines not as a process of making the unconscious conscious, but of "resolving the resistances."

As these resistances are resolved, the defenses are dropped. To borrow a concept from James F. Masterson's later works, the borderline is a compilation of defensive false selves based on fantasized projections of the patient plus the other person. As these masks are dropped, the real self emerges, healthier and more capable of facing reality than it ever dreamed was possible.

CHAPTER 7

Safety in Numbers: Group and Family Therapy

While intensive, exploratory individual psychotherapy should remain the backbone of treatment for the person with borderline personality disorder, it does not necessarily mean that it is the only treatment. As pointed out in Chapter Six, the best therapists will combine various approaches when they're working with borderline patients, especially with difficult patients. There are times during the lengthy therapeutic process when group or family therapy are extremely useful adjuncts to individual therapy and times when medication is indicated. Each patient is different. To say in advance that all patients will require medication for the first year, or that all patients under 20 years of age should be treated in family therapy, would be ridiculous. In the next two chapters, we will examine some of the possible indications for combined treatment, and their probable effects. Group and family therapy are discussed in this chapter, while medication is covered in Chapter Eight.

GROUP THERAPY

About six months ago, I decided to take a risk and introduce Madeline, one of the borderline patients I'd been working with twice a week over the past two years, into a therapy group I also run. Madeline had made quite a bit of progress in individual therapy, and seemed to have her impulsivity under control. But every time I saw her, she would relate disturbing stories about her interactions with people at work. I was getting all those stories secondhand, after the initial conflicts they had caused her had passed. I was interested in seeing her direct involvement with her peers, and the group situation seemed the best possible place. I was also hopeful that her awareness of being observed in such a situation would force her to be more observant of her own actions and reactions. I had a lot of confidence in this particular group, and was hopeful that they could naturally absorb Madeline into their midst.

During the first session, Madeline interrupted several people to draw attention to herself, then sat there pouting when the conversation shifted back to other people. At the second session, she erupted in a minor tantrum when one of her opinions was questioned. The third session consisted of Madeline plus two other group members. Clearly, Madeline's presence, if it continued, would destroy the group. So much for all the confidence I'd had in this group's ability to withstand the shock of a borderline patient, though I admit it gave me a better insight into Madeline.

Group therapy with borderline patients is very treacherous. Many a group has disbanded after such a patient was introduced. And I wouldn't be surprised if there are one or two therapists who gave up their practice after such an experience. In 1980, when I was working at an outpatient clinic in Connecticut, I ran a therapy group only for borderlines. Let me tell you, working that group was a full-time job. Not only would I do group therapy, but the next day I'd get twenty phone calls. Every patient wanted an exclusive relationship with me as their therapist, and would call the next day with some manipulative complaint, attempting to reestablish that relationship.

I repeat: *group therapy with borderline patients is very treacherous*, and unless one is in a hospital situation, where a lot more structure can be imposed before, during, and after the group session, it should be avoided at all costs. Yet many practitioners continue to champion it, either as an adjunct to individual therapy or even as the only means of treatment.

When one examines the writings of these practitioners closely, one realizes that whether or not they label themselves as such, they are practicing supportive rather than exploratory psychotherapy. They speak of the ways in which the group simulates social situations, and highlight the group's involvement in eliciting the proper social response. They speak of how the borderline patient can "borrow courage" from members of the group who have left home or gotten out of self-defeating relationships. They speak of how watching the borderline patient interact with the group offers a therapist better opportunities to confront her with her antisocial behavior. They talk about how the group setting offers a buffer, making it easier for the borderline to accept harsh facts about herself because she sees other patients accepting truths about themselves without overreacting.

As should be evident from all the above indications, the group setting might help toward reeducation of the patient, not toward resolving deeper conflicts. Yes, there is no doubt that the borderline patient needs to learn how to interact better with other people, but the group situation where the "other people" have many of the same problems is far from ideal. The borderline needing approval might "behave herself" for the group's duration, but this behavior must be viewed alongside the behavior of the heavily medicated patient, which we will explore in Chapter Eight. Remove the group's availability and the conflicts are sure to return. As is the case with most supportive psychotherapy, the patient is being put on a very short leash and expected to remain there indefinitely.

"MONSTERS" AND OTHERS: THE FAMILY UNIT

Remember Barbara, the borderline adolescent in Chapter Three who attempted suicide after a high school dance? Later, during her hospitalization, I walked into her room as she—on her own authority—was getting dressed to leave. "I've got to go home," she told me. "My mother's going crazy." I asked her if her mother had told her this. No. Her 16-year-old sister had called that morning, pleading with her to come home soon because "life's unbearable without you. Mom's at everyone's throat."

Had I known Barbara a little better, I might have pointed out how these words, "I've got to go home," echoed her words about having to get home from the dance, and how her impulsive suicide attempt had only complicated matters further. At that moment, however, I concentrated all my efforts on convincing Barbara she was too weak to go home yet. I felt it was important that, if we were ever going to establish a good therapeutic relationship, it had to be done at a time when she was separated from the rest of her family. But I also felt strongly that, if Barbara was going to emerge from treatment healthy, I would have to enlist the entire family's involvement.

Some of the strongest proponents for group therapy discuss the ways in which the unified and well-run therapy group can simulate the encouraging and supportive family unit lacking in the borderline patient's childhood. While I've yet to have any experience that proved the truth of this, such concepts force us to take a closer look at the actual family structure. Especially when working with an adolescent patient, the involvement of the parents and siblings in family therapy can be crucial in freeing the borderline from familial misconceptions and enabling her to risk change and grow into an independent person.

Like adults, borderline adolescents were at first treated in individual therapy. Gradually, as more was learned about the mother's separation anxieties and her own "borderline-type" behavior, theorists began to speculate on the usefulness of involving the mother in therapy as well. Closer examination of this mother-child relationship led eventually to attempts to include the father in therapy. In recent years, it has proven of utmost value to be able to view the borderline in her entire family setting—mother, father, siblings, and any close extended family.

Returning again to Barbara's family, we can observe a clear division between dependency and neglect. Barbara's mother had felt extremely neglected by her own parents and by her husband. Throughout the infancy of her first two daughters, she had absorbed herself in their care. But by the time they reached the rapprochement stage and wanted to set out on their own, it was just as well with the mother. She had a younger child to care for. Her husband, on the other hand, couldn't stand to have young children dependent upon him. But once they reached the toddler stage, he would enjoy activities with them, and thus provided the attention their mother no longer gave.

When Barbara reached the rapprochement stage, there was no younger child in need of her mother's attention, and her mother refused to let go. By the time Barbara was 6 or 7 years old, the rest of the family seemed to have taken it for granted that they could go off on their own, because Barbara was around to keep their mother occupied. And Barbara readily accepted the burden, and the extra attention. She began to cling to her mother and resist her father's efforts to spend time with her, and her father in turn angrily stopped trying. The sisters would spend a Sunday with their father, and come home showing off a new toy or going on and on to

Barbara about all the fun she'd missed, and Barbara developed a strong sense that she wasn't "good enough" to be included. Instead of taking the attitude that her sisters weren't "good enough" to be included in outings with their mother, Barbara saw her outings as a poor but necessary, substitute for the other things she was missing.

Necessary is the key word. Barbara might have liked to do more on her own, but she was terrified of what would happen to the rest of the family if she did. Yes, she admitted, she wanted to get "better," but she didn't want to take any chances on upsetting things, so maybe the way it was would be good enough. She saw her sessions alone with me as a betrayal of her family, and consequently had difficulty opening up to me. After all, I was an outsider; I might care about her at the moment, but if her family cut her off as a result she would be lost. Here she followed a typical borderline pattern of having to see everything as either "good" or "bad." Just as she could not love both her mother and her father, she felt that if she accepted my care she would be forced to reject the care of both her parents. It was clear that, unless I could change the basic structure of the family unit, it would be not only difficult for Barbara to change, but quite possibly dangerous.

When we look at any person with borderline personality disorder, we find someone with no sense of herself as an individual, but who constantly projects emotions onto another person. In effect, the other person plus the borderline form a single unit. All too often, when we look at the family of a borderline patient, we find a similar makeup: no family member has a sense of himself or herself as an individual; everyone is defined in relation to at least one other family member. But neither is the family unit well-defined; it has no sense of itself as a whole, and therefore no understanding that it consists of separate people who enjoy spending time together. Often such a family pattern goes back several generations.

THE FAMILY IN THERAPY

In typical borderline families, the parents seem either neglectful of or overly involved with their children. In Barbara's family, both patterns emerged. The mother had basically turned her two older daughters over to their father after the rapprochement stage, while their father lavished attention on them until they reached adolescence. When his daughters as young teenagers began to reject his care, he withdrew his support and became the authoritarian figure who was concerned only that they were home on time and weren't rude to other family members. All along, it seemed, he had been denying his own need for companionship, and his own feelings of insufficiency and rejection when his daughters set out on their own. Over recent years he had taken to spending less time at home. The family offered him nothing, so he gave nothing back.

It was only in working with the family that I was able to discover the intense bitterness in these two older children. They were bitter that support had been withdrawn from them, and jealous of the attention that Barbara still received. "If I'd pulled a suicide stunt like that," the older daughter told me, "I'll bet they'd have just let me rot in the hospital. They wouldn't put themselves out to come and visit. But for Barbara, of *course* for Barbara..."

Barbara's father also saw her suicide attempt as a stunt to get attention. And the fact that she was *getting* attention, and moreover that he was paying for it, irked him no end. Barbara's mother was overly attentive and concerned over her welfare. The more I saw mother and daughter in action together, the more I became convinced of the childishness inherent in the mother's behavior. If anything, Barbara had become the mature, responsible member of the pair, while in typical borderline fashion she denied her own neediness.

Barbara's mother was quick to acknowledge how much she needed her husband, but he had never been much of a companion for her. In lieu of his presence, she needed first one child, then another, and had finally settled for Barbara. Every other family member was involved in a process of denying their need for anyone or anything. There were frequent explosions whenever anyone was confronted directly with needing another person. In working with this family, as with other families, such rage could be trapped, held, and explored further. The family began to see how they were involved in a pattern of chain reactions. After several months, they began to be aware that at any time, any member could refuse to react and thus break the chain.

At my instigation, family members were able to discuss what they wanted and needed from each other. Both parents were able to talk about their own childhoods, what they had received and what they had been denied from their own parents. This enabled the children to see some of the repetitive patterns, as well as to declare themselves "different." I encouraged stronger bonds to develop between the parents and between the children.

Meanwhile, in individual therapy with Barbara, I was able to focus on how she was not responsible for her parents' lives. In sessions with the family, she watched her sisters become individuals without destroying the family unit, and became aware of the mistakes her parents had made both in their families of origin and in raising their children. Once she could admit that she still loved them, despite their faults, she was able to accept the good and bad within herself. She could let herself love them while remaining a person in her own right.

Because borderline adolescents such as Barbara are involved in both individual and family therapy, the growth which might have been so disastrous when they were first hospitalized becomes a natural process. Admittedly, not every family is willing to undergo such treatment, but family therapy should be encouraged wherever possible. Increasingly, as therapists have practiced family therapy with the families of adolescent borderline patients, severely disturbed family patterns have emerged. Even more surprisingly, the adolescent borderline, who has caused herself enough harm to bring the entire family to the therapist's attention, does not always emerge as the most disturbed family member. In such therapeutic situations, all members receive the help they require.

CHAPTER 8

The Proper Use of Medication

Without question, the advent of psychiatric medications has been one of the most important medical developments of the twentieth century, allowing millions of people to lead more productive and healthier lives. But the power of these medications can be a double-edged sword: when used correctly they can work miracles, but when abused they can be deadly. Given the volatile and self-destructive nature of the borderline, this potential for abuse should never be minimized. *Commandment Number One: Don't arm the borderline.*

It will come back to haunt both the doctor and the patient. Besides, she's probably fairly well-armed to begin with. One of the worst mistakes a doctor can make is to prescribe a medication with which the patient can fatally overdose, or threaten overdose. It would be as if I'd handed Angela another butcher knife the next time she came to my office.

It was 9:00 P.M. on a Saturday night, my final year as a psychiatric resident. I was almost finished with my residency, and had been invited to a dinner party at the home of a well-known physician. I have to admit I was feeling pretty good. We'd just sat down to dinner when the phone rang. It was the emergency room at the hospital. Linda, one of my borderline patients, who had been quite depressed, had just been admitted after taking half a bottle of the antidepressant, Sinequan (generic name doxepin), after several glasses of wine.

Linda was lucky this time—her sister had called right after she'd swallowed the pills, realized her voice sounded strange, and hurried over. She got her to the hospital, had her stomach pumped, and two weeks later Linda was once again coming to my office as an outpatient. But I'd learned the most important rule of psychiatric medicine for borderlines.

TOO MUCH IS NOT ENOUGH

"How do you know this patient's a borderline?" one psychiatric resident used to ask another. And the answer: "Well, she's taking eight different medications at the moment. The doctor's tried everything and doesn't know what else to do."

Despite all the literature about the tendency of borderline patients to attempt an overdose, doctors continue to keep such patients under more medication than is really needed. Patients often find themselves going to public clinics and becoming involved in test groups for particular medications. While many of these patients benefit from such therapy, the medication does not produce a permanent cure.

There is still a great deal of controversy among psychiatrists as to the applicability of using medications in treating borderline disorders, and further disagreement as to which medications are most effective. There have even been a few clinicians in recent years who have advanced the use of medication as the primary form of treatment. My own perspective is that the use of medications *combined with* intensive psychotherapy certainly has its place in treating people with borderline personality disorder.

At times, the use of medication should be the first step. When I see a borderline patient for the first time and she's experiencing a psychotic episode or extreme paranoia, then an antipsychotic medication is necessary—without it, the other forms of therapy are impossible. However, I resist the temptation to continue the medication after its usefulness has been served.

Ever since that incident with Linda, I've done my best to stay away from medications that have a dangerous overdose risk. Whenever you're working with a borderline patient, you're dealing with someone who overdoses as part of her repertoire. If you look closely at the available medications, there's often a medication that will treat the symptoms, without as great a risk. Or, when I have to administer a medication that's a potential weapon, I will prescribe a limited dosage of only a few pills. Since I'm usually seeing the patient at least once a week, I'll write frequent prescriptions for a few pills. My patient may get tired of going to the pharmacy, but she will be safe.

When working with a borderline person, you're treating a *personality disorder*. There is a basic character structure that needs to be corrected if the person is to experience any degree of health, and such a correction can only be achieved through intensive psychotherapy. Medications can be a useful tool in breaking down some of the patient's defenses that are causing her so many problems in her day-to-day life, but for the borderline patient they can never be an end in themselves. Our expectations must be realistic, and the patient symptoms should indicate the need for medication.

SYMPTOM INDICATIONS

Obviously a patient in the midst of a psychotic episode or suffering a severe anxiety attack, will require medication. But aside from such extreme states, often the symptoms the borderline complains about are modest compared with the underlying problems. There are some patients for whom the mood swings are more closely related to what is known as an "affective" or mood disorder (such as manic-depression or bipolar disorder); for these patients, the rapid shifts of mood are caused more by the mood disorder itself, and less by abandonment anxiety as they are for other borderlines. This type of patient may exhibit shifts of mood that are unconnected to other events in their lives, and usually will be extremely responsive to medication, such as lithium.

Any medication is a calculated risk for the borderline. Before prescribing medication, it's necessary to look closely at the symptoms, and to ascertain if these symptoms are usually responsive enough to the medication that it's going to be worth the risk. Not only is such a patient prone to overdose, she is especially sensitive to the effects of even normal doses of medication. And given the borderline's inclination for denial and avoidance of assuming responsibility for her actions, she will frequently attribute the next depression or panic attack to being a side-effect of the medication, when such is not the case. We must also keep in mind that these medications may interact dangerously with other substances, such as alcohol, and I would want to be absolutely certain that my new borderline patient does not also have problems with drinking or illegal drugs before writing a prescription.

In addition to the medications for depression and anxiety, which are listed below, it has been found that some borderline patients who find it especially difficult to control their impulsive actions respond well to anticonvulsant medications. Frequent lack of controlled behavior can be caused by seizures. In these cases, electroencephalogram (EEG) and sophisticated brain-mapping procedures may uncover physiological problems. These patients merit trial on antiseizure medications, such as phenytoin sodium (brand name Dilantin), carbamazepine (Tegretol), and valproic acid.

DEPRESSION

Depression is the most common complaint of borderlines, and it's often useful to treat them with antidepressant medications. Given the borderline's rapid mood shifts and pessimistic view of life as "all good" or "all bad" to begin with, a physician shouldn't be too quick to prescribe antidepressants. The general way in which the borderline handles her life leads to a lot of stress and causes depression, and sometimes such depressions are better worked out through psychotherapy alone. But when you have someone who's gotten depressed and suicidal and the depression has been going on for more than a couple of weeks, then antidepressants are usually indicated.

Trazodone (brand name Desyrel) is one antidepressant I prescribe often because it's very difficult to overdose on it—people have swallowed a hundred of them without serious consequences. I have found that some borderline patients with depression need higher doses of antidepressant medication, and even then may only respond after many weeks (although the usual response to an antidepressant for depression not associated with borderline disorder is two to three weeks). In addition to trazodone, other common antidepressants include imipramine, desipramine, and fluoxetine (prozac), although the potential of overdose must always be considered.

Some doctors have had success prescribing monoamine (MAO) inhibitor medications (such as phenelzine and tranylcypromine) for depression. The MAO inhibitors are excellent for depression; however they can present problems for the borderline patient. These medications can be very dangerous and even deadly when combined with foods or drinks containing a substance called tyramine. Tyramine can be found in a large number of common foods, including aged meats and cheeses, wine, and chocolate. In addition, some common medications that may increase blood pressure (such as many over-the-counter cold and hay fever preparations) when combined with MAO inhibitors may cause a dangerously high increase in blood pressure. Because of the potential for serious food and drug interactions, I generally refrain from administering MAO inhibitors to borderline patients.

CRISIS INTERVENTIONS

Low doses of antipsychotic medications, such as thioridazine (Mellaril) or chlorpromazine (Thorazine), or the antianxiety class of medications called benzodiazepines can be extremely useful in crisis situations. Common benzodiazepine medications include diazepam (Valium) and lorazepam (Ativan). These sedative medications, prescribed on an as-needed basis, can sometimes effectively reduce the patient's anxiety and agitation. During times of crisis, the borderline patient is particularly susceptible to experiencing brief psychotic episodes, and the antipsychotics can be extremely useful in helping her to maintain her hold on reality. A sense of anxiety and confusion can, with the help of medication, be replaced by a calmer attitude, even when the specific problems have not yet been resolved. As with many other psychiatric disorders, often the patients with the most severe symptoms will have the greatest response.

The borderline patient who experiences acute anxiety or panic in certain situations, such as riding in a car or elevator, will often feel better under medication; if the medication is stopped, the anxiety will reappear. In general, antianxiety medication should be prescribed only in extreme situations, not just to make the day-to-day stresses bearable. We must at all times remember that the most successful therapy for borderlines is intensive psychotherapy over a sustained period of time.

Except for the antidepressant medication, which often needs

to be prescribed regularly for a sustained period, I seldom put patients on a long-term medication schedule. My experience with borderline patients indicates that often they won't maintain a regular medication schedule. Often they will let large amounts of the medication accumulate, and can either accidentally or deliberately overdose. For patients taking the antipsychotic and antianxiety medications, I recommend that they carry one or two pills in their pocket, and use the medication on an "as needed" basis, to cut short moments of severe agitation and stress.

As will be explored in Chapter Nine, during extreme decompensations (such as suicidal behavior, psychotic episodes) it's sometimes best to put the patient in the hospital for a brief period, where high-risk medications can be administered under extremely controlled conditions. The psychiatrist at this point is working under the assumption that the condition will immediately respond to the combination of the structured hospital environment and the medication, and that the patient can be released after a brief period and maintained either without medication, or with a medication that is not as dangerous.

THE ALL-IMPORTANT INTRODUCTION

Janine was another patient who entered therapy in early 1984, during a post-abandonment depression. She had been in therapy twice before with different doctors; the last time had been over two years ago. She followed the usual borderline pattern of feeling better after a while, dropping out of treatment, and then calling another doctor when the pressures and depression once again became too much for her. Over the past ten years, she'd been through a number of relationships, lasting from two to six months, and had become increasingly frightened by her inability to, as she put it, "make anything work right."

I saw Janine twice a week for about three months, and was impressed with both her intelligence and her progress in therapy. I was, frankly, surprised when she called late on a Sunday night, spoke to my answering service, and asked for an emergency appointment for the next morning. She was distraught when she entered my office, yet her sarcasm and irritability also seemed at its height. It took quite a bit of patience and self-control before I learned that she'd run into a former boyfriend at the theater the night before. The boyfriend was with a beautiful young woman, and they appeared to be very much in love. It simply seemed too much of a shock for Janine to be able to handle, and I sensed her getting worse by the minute. Before she left my office, I wrote out a prescription for a low dose of a benzodiazepine, to decrease her agitation.

Even though I had given her my home telephone number, Janine called my answering service to say she wouldn't be able to make her next appointment. For the appointment after that, she arrived a half hour late. This time she was angry, and her anger was directed at me, but I couldn't discern a clear pattern of what had caused the anger, and her quips at me seemed unconnected to anything that had happened. I asked if she'd taken the medication, and she broke out in a deep, mocking laugh. It wasn't until the middle of the next session that I had a clue as to what had caused the still-present anger. "You had no right to just toss me aside like that," Janine screamed. "I thought you cared about me."

Suddenly it was all too clear. Like other borderlines, Janine had entered therapy in the hopes that I would provide the nurturing experience she had never gotten from any of her previous relationships. One of the reasons she had progressed as far as she did in the first months of treatment was that she immediately accepted me as a person who cared more than anyone else, and my introduction of medication into the therapy had been seen as a cold, inhuman brushoff.

On the surface, she seemed so stable that I believed that

she could cope with a prescription. But her reaction illustrates that it may take a borderline several months or longer to trust the therapist enough that they don't view the sudden introduction of medication as one more effort to control them. A physician must be aware of this, reassure the patient that she is not being abandoned, and spell out exactly what could be expected from the medication.

Working with *any* psychiatric patient, a physician should take time to explain the need for a particular medication, and impress upon the patient the necessity that they take it precisely as prescribed. With many patients this discussion can be kept to a minimum. As I told Janine: "I can see what you're going through, this experience is really hard for you, and I'm going to prescribe some pills that will make you feel better for the next few weeks." That is usually not enough of an explanation for most borderlines.

When introduced properly, the need for medication and the patient's understanding of that need can be made as essential to the therapeutic process as are transference or interpretation. The borderline's main problem is her impulsiveness, and one of the worst mistakes a therapist could make would be to let the patient believe he is impulsively deciding upon a medication which might or might not work. By discussing possible side effects in advance, the therapist leaves less room for the patient to attribute imaginary or unrelated symptoms to the effect of the medication. By discussing what he is hoping to gain with the addition of the medication, he is leaving less room for the patient to feel cheated and "bad" because she did not immediately become a "good, healthy" person. Such unrealistically high hopes left unexplained and unfulfilled are one of the quickest ways to drive a borderline patient away from continued treatment.

At the other end of the spectrum is the borderline patient who is attached to her conflicted, tumultuous state. I stated above that a sense of anxiety and confusion can, under medication, be replaced by a calmer attitude. Many borderline persons have never experienced such a calmness before, and they don't quite know what to make of it. They will complain that they feel "dead" (as opposed to the common complaint of feeling "empty"), they will complain that they can't get up energy to do anything, that they lack spontaneity. Many a psychiatrist will accept these words at face value, and discontinue the medication without trusting his own judgment that the patient does not seem "lifeless" to him. Once again, proper introduction to the medication would not have prevented this state, but it might have helped the patient to handle it better.

As with so many other issues involved when working with borderline patients, the more supports and stabilizing factors there are in a patient's life outside therapy, the more she can be expected to comply with the medication properly, experience its benefits, and suffer less from its side effects. Those patients who lack external supports will place all the more value upon the psychiatrist's continued presence; in such cases he must take extra care to reassure the patient of his availability, and then be prepared to make good on his promise.

CHAPTER 9

When Hospitalization Is Necessary

I was the psychiatric resident on call at the general hospital one night in December 1978. It was three in the morning and I was attempting to get a little sleep when my beeper went off. "Psych case E.R. 103" the operator droned. When I got down to Emergency, I noticed that several nurses and doctors were giving me suspicious-looking grins. I was more than a bit confused by this reception, but passed it off as my being still half asleep.

As I drew the curtains on Room 103, I saw Lorna, a beautiful woman dressed in a hospital gown and sitting calmly on the stretcher. I took her history and did a mental status examination. She explained that she'd been in the hospital many times before for "depression," but she felt okay right now. She added that she'd had a fight with her lover earlier in the evening, but she didn't care about him any more. After an hour of questions, I was still baffled as to why I had been awakened at 3:00 A.M. to care for her. Finally, I asked her directly: "Why are you here?"

Still smiling, Lorna slowly unfastened her gown, revealing

a large safety pin perfectly clasped through her left breast. No, she no longer felt like hurting herself, really, she was fine. But then again, she always felt better in the safe, sterile hospital environment. Her self-destructive action had assured she would be taken care of.

I had no choice but to admit her to the psychiatric unit. The next day I learned that Lorna's boyfriend had kicked her out. She said this made her angry, but at the same time she felt too empty to feel much of anything. She pinned herself, and felt real again. Then she called the ambulance.

It never ceases to amaze hospital staff how quickly the raging, hysterical, suicidal, psychotic borderline patient quiets down once she finds herself within the confines of the hospital walls. This can be better explained if we return for a moment to Chapter Two. It was discussed there how the borderline who senses herself in a stable, supportive relationship will function with a fair degree of normalcy. At the first indications of possible abandonment, anxiety takes over, leading to various acting-out episodes and manipulative suicide attempts. It is only upon what is perceived by the borderline to be actual loss of the supporting object that she loses hold on reality, and is prone to psychotic episodes. It was also pointed out how quickly the borderline can face reality once again as soon as the support network is reestablished. In the case above, as often happens with borderline patients, the hospital is viewed as offering such support.

For some borderlines, the prospect of being taken care of will be enough to keep them quiet for some time. As Lorna said, she'd had a fight with her boyfriend earlier in the evening, but that didn't matter any more. The "all good" borderline is fighting off memory of her "badness." For many other patients, the rapprochement crisis begins again: the moment they sense support they fear engulfment. The patient who was psychotic in the emergency room calms down as a result of the staff's efforts, then a short time later becomes paranoid, enraged, or at best anxious at being held against her will. There will be manipulative attempts to gain control of staff members, water pitchers thrown against walls, windows shattered. But no one can afford to forget the crisis that brought her to the hospital in the first place.

When the situation in everyday life is perceived as frustrating enough, borderlines tend toward the dramatic in their acting-out behavior. When the borderline person who is not receiving psychiatric help feels the pressures becoming unbearable, she will perform some act that ensures her of hospitalization and proper care, just as Lorna did. These patients cannot be put on a clinic's waiting list; they are crying out for help in the moment (or they have been crying out for some time, and no one has responded).

THE INITIAL THERAPEUTIC BOND

When the borderline person has her first "break"—performs her first act self-destructive enough to land her in the hospital—a thirty-day hospitalization may be essential. For many a frantic, driven borderline patient, the hospital will be the first stable environment she has experienced in a long time, and as such it offers the patient a rare opportunity to begin to understand her situation and work with the therapist toward some basic changes. In that month you can really establish a therapeutic bond, especially when the same psychiatrist is going to be treating her later as an outpatient. You can make some progress, which could mean the difference between life and death.

ADOLESCENT HOSPITALIZATION

This first hospitalization is even more important in the case of an adolescent, where the act which prompted hospitalization is often part of a larger pattern. Unless the pattern can be broken, there is little chance of improvement. Also, as pointed out in Chapter Three, keeping the adolescent in the hospital is a powerful method of indicating to the family the importance of what has happened. In some families, there's a tendency to deny the symptoms of an adolescent borderline—much of that denial is broken down by the significance of having an adolescent in the hospital. It's a very important beginning and it can be instrumental in getting the adolescent into sustained treatment. For adolescents and adults alike, the first hospitalization and subsequent therapy sets the tone for everything that happens later.

Ideally, for maximum therapeutic benefit after that first incident, the patient would remain hospitalized for a period of three to six months. But many insurance policies will only cover thirty days. In addition, many borderline patients after thirty days are often capable of benefitting from outpatient therapy.

There are some theorists who disagree with me, recommending original hospitalizations of a year or more for borderline patients. Supportive and behavioral therapists, in particular, stress the hospital's role in helping the patient develop a better self-image. *Advice, direction,* and *control* seem to be the key words. They have emphasized the usefulness of long-term hospitalization as a means of providing job training or permitting patients to complete their education, and stress that the bond formed with staff members and other patients is crucial in helping patients later adapt to a community outside the hospital. They stress the use of the supportive hospital setting as a "holding environment" and a substitute for parenting which has not been "good-enough."

But even many of these theorists acknowledge that, especially for the adolescent, a long hospital stay might be an act of vengeance against her parents who are, after all, forced to pay for this, and forced to deal with the public "shame" of mental illness. They are careful to point out the borderline patient's reluctance to leave the hospital after a long stay, and the tendency of such patients to worsen on discharge and perform acts that will quickly return them to the hospital. They stress that discharge of the borderline patient must be done with caution, the patient must be given to understand that the hospital door is always open, that she will always be able to return if necessary, that the staff will always be there to welcome her.

I object to such a practice. While I see the first stay in the hospital as an education, any bonds established should be between the patient and the *therapist*, not between the patient and the hospital. The patient should never become dependent upon the hospital. While there are many positive aspects to a longer hospital stay, whenever you're treating a borderline patient, you're working with someone who's terrified of abandonment. You have to be thinking about issues of termination—in this case the release from the hospital, later the termination of therapy—from Day One. Otherwise you have a much larger problem on your hands.

To reiterate: if one enters treatment in a crisis situation, I recommend a thirty-day hospitalization at first, then briefer hospitalizations to deal with crisis situations. For those borderlines who are functioning fairly well and enter treatment as outpatients, often brief hospitalizations in times of crisis will be sufficient.

BRIEF HOSPITALIZATIONS IN TIMES OF CRISIS

In recent years, as more has been learned about borderline personality disorder, many hospitals have established specific borderline units, geared to keeping patients seven to ten days, working closely with the patient's therapist, and dealing with the immediate crisis. The hospital unit admitting the borderline patient must be highly structured and well organized, in order to contain the borderline's self-destructive behavior. The staff is especially equipped to keep close watch over the patient who is highly medicated, or taking a medication which must be administered with extreme care, and whose effects must be closely observed.

The members of the hospital staff should meet the same requirements as the therapist who works well with borderlines: they must be comfortable with their own aggressive tendencies so that they do not react to the patient's anger, and they must be in touch with their own separation anxieties. Separation anxieties might be extreme for the hospitalized borderline who, despite the fact that she is continuing to see her therapist, might still feel like the bad, abandoned child. We have already seen this syndrome in Chapter Eight, where Janine was not properly prepared to accept a new medication, and believed it to be the therapist's rejection of her as a person.

No psychiatrist should ever promise to keep a borderline patient out of the hospital. The possibility of brief hospitalizations as the therapy progresses should be discussed with outpatients at the beginning of therapy, then reiterated as treatment progresses. "I can't help you unless you're willing to help yourself" is the basic text. "If you continue your self-destructive behavior with frequent suicide attempts, abusing alcohol or drugs, then my hands are tied. If I have to continually intervene in crisis situations in order to save your life, then we're never going to be able to face any of the larger issues together."

I repeat that the therapist is not the patient's mother. Especially when the borderline patient is not involved in a supportive relationship outside the therapeutic situation, the therapist who frequently intervenes in life-saving situations becomes the target for future acting-out. Thus manipulative behavior is unconsciously encouraged. While transference should always be a goal of the therapy, the therapist must also be certain that his unavailability when a patient calls or inability to schedule an emergency appointment two hours later does not precipitate manipulative self-destruction.

For a neurotic patient, the acting-out of transference feelings sometimes offers new insights into herself. For the borderline patient, acting-out is almost always a resistance to accepting and appreciating the therapist's role. Any real transference for the borderline patient must be on a level the patient has not experienced before: the therapist who withstands their aggression and abuse, and at the same time sets a limit upon actual manipulation. In effect, these limits are another way of assisting the patient in dealing with the abandonment crisis and preparing her to eventually terminate psychotherapy.

Though they seldom admit it at the time, most borderline patients appreciate such a policy. People have been either giving in to them or running away from their aggression far too long. If I didn't continually point out the inappropriateness of the patient's rage, it would be as if I were condoning it. It would be as if this were the young child with mother looking the other way, saying it's okay, let her have her tantrum, she'll get over it, she doesn't have the power to really hurt herself. G. J. Sarwer-Foner has put it better than I can: "Indeed, the more regressed the patient, the more important is the physician's attitude that the patient is not a helpless mobile, but is an interested and at least potentially able participant in the therapeutic process."

As discussed in Chapter Six, I also take care to continually point out to each patient how disruptive self-destructive behavior is going to be to her life. I ignore the patient who comes into the office on Monday morning with her wrists bandaged and tells me, "Well, it was a hard weekend, I really thought Johnny was going to leave me. But I feel better now, much better." As a therapist, it's my duty to throw it back on the real issue: "Look what this means in terms of your day to day life. I'm sending you to the hospital for a few days and you're going to be without Johnny anyway, aren't you? You should have thought about your actions before giving in to your impulses again."

Some patients have a higher threshold. I guess it all comes down to: how deep was the cut? What level of self-destruction sends you into the hospital? A patient can make a slight carving, but if I know they've made progress with their therapy, then hospitalization may not be required. It's peculiar to each patient, as you get to know them you understand what constitutes dangerousness for that particular patient.

THE DOWNHILL CURVE

It is one of the basic tenets of psychotherapy that often a patient has to get worse before she gets better. This is particularly true of the "apparently competent" borderline who enters therapy as an outpatient, feeling somewhat disturbed or depressed, but not understanding the cause of the disturbance. All her relationships and friendships thus far have been on a superficial level, and even though she appears to lead a normal life, this has suddenly proved insufficient. Such a person has probably spent her life running away from conflict. She has avoided introspection for fear of unleashing aggressive tendencies, and with foreknowledge of the psychological pain her aggression might cause. But as we saw in Chapter Six, the resistances to the unconscious must be dissolved if intense, exploratory psychotherapy is to effect a basic structural change in the patient's overall makeup.

Sometimes the patient's resistances produce what might be best considered a therapeutic stalemate. The patient is not any worse than before, but neither is any real progress being made toward resolving the resistances. The patient once so anxious for help becomes passive. She listens to what the therapist says, but is basically unwilling to reveal much that's been going on in her day to day life, so she doesn't leave the therapist much room for interpretation or confrontation. Such a stalemate can occur at the beginning of treatment, or at any time during the therapy. Often it will take place after a major leap has been made in the therapeutic bond. The patient has shared new material, exposed herself, made herself vulnerable. She now fears that either the therapist will use the material to exploit her, or he will turn away from her now that she has revealed how "bad" she is. Possibly the revelations she has made to the therapist make her feel calmer, and she's now afraid of reverting to a state of dreaded emptiness. Instead of going along with the good feeling, she impulsively acts to destroy it.

Again here, we must recall the borderline's masochistic yet basic fear of engulfment. All her life she has run away from love, concern, honesty, and understanding. As Otto F. Kernberg has pointed out, the therapist who is working with a patient who suddenly becomes unresponsive, has a brief psychotic episode, or begins self-destructive behavior soon after new material has been explored "is facing the activation of the deepest levels of human aggression." At such times, Kernberg contends, the patient reveals "an almost conscious sense of triumph in defeating his own efforts, a triumph over the therapist, whose impotence is reconfirmed every day as impossible situations develop and disaster is courted." At this point, Kernberg recommends the therapist assume a strong analytic, confrontational approach. "It is essential that the therapist interpret the unconscious (and sometimes conscious) rage at him expressed in the patient's playing Russian roulette in his daily life."

Since often this "crisis" was precipitated by uncovering the events of early childhood, the patient must continually be reminded that, whatever its usefulness might have been in the past, the things that are happening right now in her life do not entitle her to this much rage. She must continually be urged to recognize the way her aggression is limiting her ability to function in the here and now.

Placing such a patient in the hospital for a brief period does more than simply prevent further self-destructive behavior. Having more people around to relate to can also be a means of allaying some of the patient's anxiety that the therapist is one person attempting to control her. His availability as the only supportive person in her life is negated, and his presence itself becomes less subject to distortion. If the therapist has repeatedly discussed the possible need for further hospitalization with the patient since the beginning of therapy, at times like this just the suggestion of hospitalization might help the patient regain perspective and greatly reduce her anxieties.

ABANDONMENT REGRESSIONS

In 1984, Judith Rossner's best-selling novel, *August*, was seemingly in the hands of half the people I saw riding busses or sitting on park benches. Rossner focuses on the lives of two women over a period of several years: Dawn, a young college student and artist involved in intensive psychotherapy and Dawn's analyst, Dr. Lulu Shinefeld, who is herself a single mother. Like other human beings, Dr. Shinefeld needs a vacation every year, and like other New York City therapists, she tends to go away every August.

If nothing else, *August* was instrumental in enlightening the American public to how difficult it is for the person involved in intense psychoanalysis to suddenly find herself left to her own devices for a period of time. To a greater or lesser extent, many patients under psychiatric care tend to regress during periods when their therapist cannot treat them. Such behavior is even more common in the case of the borderline patient whose entire life is controlled by a fear of abandonment.

Every time I'm tempted to pat myself on the back for the progress being made with a particular borderline patient, I recall Angela idealizing me as "Dr. Pierce." One of the most important battles all borderline patients face is to be able to accept other people for what they are, not what they would like them to be. And the psychiatrist is frequently the first "real person" the patient must relate to. The borderline patient eventually has to accept his departure as more than an "abandonment" issue.

There are many patients for whom separation anxieties are present from the start. If you see such patients three times a week, you frequently find they perform well Monday through Friday, then go on alcoholic or eating binges over the weekend, or use the weekends as a perfect time for dangerous promiscuity, reckless driving, shopping sprees, and anything else that has been a self-defeating pattern for a period before they entered therapy.

Here again, this is often due to the patient's unconsciously running away from any deep probe of her unconscious. The therapist has begun to lead her closer to issues she does not want to face, then "abandoned" her, and she sees her self-destructive behavior as punishment, not of herself but of the analyst. As Harold F. Searles has described it, such a patient is "burning the other person in effigy within himself; he keeps throwing the internalized analyst upon the latter's face, within himself." As pointed out in Chapter Six, this self-destructive behavior that continues through the first months of treatment must be, for all intents and purposes, halted before the real therapeutic process can begin.

As we saw in the preceding pages, the development of a good therapeutic relationship does not necessarily mean an end to all acting-out behavior. There will be times when issues touched upon in the therapy itself will provoke silence or impulsive, foolish actions. There will be relationships which will inevitably develop outside the therapy which will often set off a regression for the borderline patient: the presence of a new lover or rejection by an old one, a visit or even a telephone call from a patient's parents, the need to sell a car or move to a new apartment, a change of jobs, even a promotion at work, can greatly upset the structured routine in which the borderline patient has managed to function with such apparent success.

And just when everything else was going so well, life seemed so organized, here is the therapist going away for a month. Obviously, I always have someone covering for me when I go away—sometimes it's a doctor who will continue to treat the patient on a regular basis, sometimes it's just the number of a doctor they can call if they're experiencing panic or just want to talk to someone. Yet despite the best efforts, any therapist who does a lot of work with borderline patients can expect that he'll return from a vacation to find that at least one of them has been hospitalized during his absence. There are some therapists who even remind the patient before they go away that if their behavior becomes dangerous enough they're going to end up in the hospital (or as we saw at the start of the chapter, use the hospital's "open door" policy as a supportive alternative). That's something I'd never advise. Just mentioning the hospital to the borderline patient before you leave almost sets up a situation where they'll end up hospitalized.

Not infrequently, as the prospect of actual termination of therapy draws nearer, the patient's anxiety will be at such a height that she'll require hospitalization for a brief period. Once again, the availability of hospital staff provides a buffer to ease the reliance she places upon the therapist alone, and often this brief hospitalization near the end of treatment prepares her for the necessary termination. If the patient is well enough to end therapy, then what is being discussed here has been reiterated over a period of years and comes as no great shock. As I mentioned at the start of this chapter, when you're working with borderline patients, you're dealing with the prospect of termination from practically the first session. It's not going to do anyone any good to have the patient so reliant upon either the therapist or the hospital that she's never going to venture forth on her own.

CHAPTER 10

What Can We Expect?

"I meet wonderful people through my job," says Ellen, who's been publicity director of a large publishing house for nearly four years. "I guess that's where the emphasis is for me these days: doing a good job in a situation that's challenging and forces me to give everything I have to it, and feeling good about myself as a result of that. Being friendly with people is part of my work, and I can handle that really well. I don't have to sleep with someone just to prove I exist. I know who I am, and I'm not complaining." When Ellen entered therapy in 1982, she was 25 years old, had held several different secretarial jobs, was extremely promiscuous, and with a potentially serious drinking problem. I saw her twice a week through 1986. Her promiscuity's definitely a thing in the past, and she can even laugh about it. She never takes more than an occasional glass of wine with dinner. She's also reestablished connections with her family, whom she'd had nothing to do with for the five years preceding her entering therapy. Often she enjoys taking her sister's two children out for weekends.

Cassie turned 28 years old last April, and left therapy with my approval after three years as a birthday present to herself. When she entered therapy, she earned barely enough to live on by taking temporary clerk-typist jobs. As she put it: "I know it's not going to last, so I don't have to try very hard. I do what they pay me to, take the money, and get the hell out of there." She seemed to change lovers (both male and female) almost as rapidly, and for many of the same reasons: it won't last, so why bother? I met a few of her lovers when they picked her up at my office, and I, too, was hopeful they wouldn't last. She drifted toward people who held low-level jobs and seemed to earn self-esteem by continually degrading her. Thirteen months before she left therapy, she began a live-in relationship with a divorced salesman who seemed gentle and somewhat protective of her. Louis said at the time he'd never marry again, and that seems to have freed Cassie to commit herself to the relationship without being frightened it will all turn bad. Around the same time, she accepted a full-time job in an insurance office, where she still works.

Borderlines can fall in love, but they can't stay in love, I stated in Chapter Four. That's the main key to health as I see it: the ability to have a normal relationship in the face of both real and imagined frustrations. To unite the good and bad in yourself and other people. And this applies not just to love relationships, but to everything: home, work, friends, family.

When we look at Ellen or Cassie today, we don't necessarily see good all-American women that we want to use as models for our children, but we don't see anything that frightens us, either. Many of the people she works with think of Ellen as lonely, but Ellen doesn't see herself that way, she's learned to be comfortable with herself. She knows herself well enough to trust what she wants and doesn't want, and she's not easily pressured by what other people think of as normal. When she spends time with a man, she does so because she wants to, not because she needs to. She no longer has to have someone to lean on, so she's much better able to enjoy herself and live in the here and now.

For Cassie the ability to stay put—both in a relationship and at her job—has been the major development in her life. At work she receives the support of her peers and goes home knowing she's done a good day's work for more than just the money; at home she receives more love than she ever thought possible, and she's no longer afraid of accepting it.

Both these women have fought a long, hard battle to get to where they are now, in therapy as well as in their day-to-day lives. They've been willing to take chances, they've been hospitalized for brief periods during treatment when things were at their worst, but they've come out on top. They're not necessarily going to turn into the most popular or successful people in the world, but then who would be? They're just sensitive, caring people who have achieved a comfortable level of stability. They're independent adults who move about at will, based on adult decisions, no longer screaming children who feel "entitled" and "deprived." They're not afraid of competing or succeeding. They're able to be open and trusting with other people, they can get angry without fearing retaliation, and their anger is based on current events instead of past deprivations or fantasies. They don't recall me as a "Dr. Pierce" or Dr. Freud, but as an imperfect doctor who struggled to help them.

That doesn't mean they're not still extremely vulnerable, but their impulsive acts are few and far between, and not nearly as manipulative or self-defeating as they once were. Taking into account such factors as the person's I.Q. and other natural assets, as well as her upbringing and the expectations drilled into her since childhood, both these women seem to have progressed as far as society might have expected them to. Both would be likely to describe themselves as "happy"—the key word which, as we saw in Chapter Two, had not previously been in their vocabularies.

As I mentioned in Chapter One, there tends to be a

general muting of the symptoms of borderline personality disorder as people get older. If only just because some of the neurons in our cortex are decreasing in number, there seems to be a flattening-out of personality characteristics in general. A patient diagnosed as borderline during adolescence or in her early twenties who does not receive treatment will probably remain distinctly borderline for the next ten years. Around age thirty, there seem to be some subtle changes: they might gradually seek out better jobs, relationships might last a bit longer, though they will still be tumultuous. Maybe half of these people will learn to interact well with other people and establish support networks that would have been thought inconceivable ten years before. While they would still probably be diagnosed as borderline, and still be unlikely to refer to themselves as happy, they are less confused about their identities and tend not to be as defensive or impulsive in their actions.

In 1986, Dr. Michael Stone conducted a long-term follow-up study on how patients previously diagnosed as borderline had adjusted once they'd left therapy. Dr. Stone reestablished contact with 254 borderline patients who had been hospitalized at the New York State Psychiatric Institute between 1963 and 1976, and treated with intensive psychotherapy. The patients had all been hospitalized for at least three months, with an average stay of just over a year. Several of the patients had no borderline or other psychological symptoms when they were discharged, and have remained well ever since. Two have even become presidents of large corporations.

Stone also reports a number of borderline patients who stayed in the hospital only for the minimum period of three months, did not describe their stay as a "rewarding" experience, did not seek further therapy within the next ten years, yet still ended up "recovered": they include a musician, a lawyer, a professor, and a religious leader. Stone attributes their recovery to the hospitalization during a critical, self-destructive period, plus "innate powers of recuperation related to personal assets such as courage, perseverance, and industriousness."

And then there's Phyllis. Phyllis was 19 when she was hospitalized after a suicide attempt in 1981. She'd been thrown out of the small, strict women's college she attended, for having snuck different men into her room on several occasions. Afraid of her parents finding out, she'd gone to live with a man who had recently become physically abusive. She'd slit her wrists after one of their frequent arguments. Phyllis stayed in the hospital for thirty days, then continued therapy with me as an outpatient. She got an apartment and began taking night courses at a local university. The next fall she entered school on a full-time basis, sharing her apartment with a female classmate, and seeing me three times a week. By the time she left therapy in late 1985, she had graduated college and had a position as dress buyer for a local department store, a job she'd wanted very badly. She'd been dating the same man for about six months, and felt good about the relationship continuing.

Five months ago, Phyllis called unexpectedly. She told me she was going through some "big changes" and asked to set up a few appointments "just to help me sort things out and make certain I don't do anything impulsive or crazy." She still had her gloves on when she arrived for her first appointment, and made a big show of removing them to reveal her wedding ring. She'd been married almost a year, she said, to the same man she'd been dating when she left therapy. They were thinking about having children now. That's why she'd come to see me. "I'm frightened," she said. "I don't want to repeat the same patterns all over again, I don't want to raise children who are going to be afraid of doing anything on their own. Do you think I can handle it?"

I looked at the calm, smiling woman in front of me. Yes, I was fairly certain she could handle it. But it's not the therapist's job to provide a patient with easy answers or directives, but to assist them in coming to their own conclusions. I smiled, offering what I hoped was a hint of my thoughts, and suggested we spent a few sessions looking closely at how she'd changed and grown over the past few years.

For one thing, I was anxious to get her to pinpoint her fears. "That the children will grow up hating me," was her quick response. Was she afraid for herself, that she'd go back to being what she'd been eight years ago? "No," Phyllis answered. "I've hit bottom, I already know what it was like there, and I'm not afraid of that. I conquered my fears and emerged better for them once, and I can always do it again if I have to. No, it's only the children I'm afraid for."

After that, we spent two sessions talking about her job. She was now a top buyer for three departments. She really enjoyed her work. "I guess that's part of why Jeff and I have such a good relationship," she said. "We each have our own interests, there's no chance of my getting too dependent on him, sometimes it's as if he takes as much pride in my work as I do." Jeff, meanwhile, was vice-president at one of the large corporations.

Otto F. Kernberg's statement that, in order to prevent borderline personality disorder, children need a maximum availability of the mother during the first two years of life kept going through my mind. I also knew that many years had passed since Kernberg had first voiced that concept. More women have sought careers, and succeeded to an extent that society didn't think possible back in the 1950s. And along with those changes, borderline personality disorder has been diagnosed more and more frequently. If this trend is not going to continue, then someone has to find a way for working mothers and divided families to foster more emotional stability in their children.

If Phyllis were a typical "textbook" case, I might have helped her to realize that her husband made a good salary, and they didn't really need her income to supplement it. I might have encouraged her to take off work for the first two years of her child's life, or at least encouraged her to work only part time. But would that really be in her (or her child's) best interests?

The more I listened to Phyllis talk about her work, the more convinced I became that her feeling of pride in her job was an important factor in her life at this point. Take away the job, and many of her old questions about her own self-worth were liable to arise. Sure, I could help her to see the true value of the love she received from her husband, but one of the first things she'd pointed out to me was how an important part of their relationship was that they each had their own lives. Whether or not this was true, Phyllis deeply believed that. It also seemed, in her case, that if she had nothing to do all day but stay home with her child, many of the old rapprochement fears would reassert themselves.

In his later work, James F. Masterson rephrases Kernberg's original concept of "good-enough" mothering to include "the emotional health of the mother, the emotional health of the child, the age of the child when the mother leaves to work, the type of relationship between the mother and the child, and the adequacy of a substitute to take care of the child's needs." I asked Phyllis how she proposed to handle child care.

"I've thought about that," Phyllis said. "I've thought about it a lot. What I'm hoping is to be able stay home for about three months when the baby's first born. But I know I'm going to have to go back to work soon after that, otherwise I'll go crazy." There was a little laugh as she said the word *crazy*, making it obvious that she was using the word as calmly as anyone else would, not fearing it or seeing it as a possibility.

"I have a few friends with small children," she continued. "They've hired sitters pretty much full time during the day. I'm not talking about ten different teenagers, like my mother used to hire, I'm talking about one person who works from eight to six four or five days a week. The baby will get to know her, and she'll be really good with the baby or I won't hire her. It'll be almost like having a mother around. Maybe even better, since she'll be used to working with children, and probably less afraid to let a child learn for herself than I would be. At least till the child's three years old or so. Then maybe I'd like to send her to nursery school part time, to get her used to being around other children, and hire the sitter the rest of the time I'm working."

I had to admit that, if she was careful about who she hired, that might be the best answer for Phyllis and her child. When we speak these days about "good-enough mothering" perhaps we are also speaking about the *quality* of the time and attention that both the mother and father are able to devote to the child when they *aren't* working. If both parents spend time with the children, and enjoy rather than begrudge that time, then their sense of enjoyment and love will more than likely foster the children's growth and development.

With all the changes in society over the past twenty or thirty years, we are forced to admit that many mothers who desperately want children also want or need to keep working outside the home. And not all of them can afford full-time help like Phyllis and her husband could. Phyllis herself admitted that most of her salary would probably go to paying the sitter, but still felt it was better that way.

Not all couples are as well-to-do financially as Phyllis and Jeff seemed to be. If the parents can't afford that, then what? Daycare. Over 65 percent of American mothers now work outside the home.

But even within daycare, there are any number of options available. Selma Fraiberg, in her book *Every Child's Birthright— In Defense of Mothering* (Basic Books, 1977), indicated that daycare of six hours or less per day can be well tolerated by children 3 years or older. More than 6 hours and the child can become very cross. The questions you must ask yourself include: How many hours of daycare will be necessary? How many children will be in the daycare setting, and what are their ages? How many adults? Obviously, when you have one adult caring for ten children under a year old, or one adult caring for twenty children all under 5 years old, you don't have the best setting for one child to receive much individual attention. I have another patient whose daughter entered a variation of daycare when she was 5 months old. But it was in the home of a young woman who had a happy marriage and two school-age children of her own, then cared for three or four others. At most, there were six children there, and my friend's daughter was the youngest. The child not only received care and attention from the sitter, but by the time she was a year old she'd established incredibly loving bonds with the sitter's two children, ages 6 and 8.

And, one more factor that hadn't yet crossed Phyllis' mind: what about other children? Many couples today hope to have more than one child. The young child going through a rapprochement crisis who suddenly finds her mother preoccupied with the care of a new infant is bound to feel deprived of her mother's attention. True, many of us as happy adults today lived through such an experience, but can we really look back on our childhoods and say they were ideal? We want better for our own children, we want to build a better society, which is one of the reasons that women have entered the job marketplace in the attempt to define themselves as individuals. If we are really striving for this ideal, then children even in those families where the mother remains at home would probably be spaced at least three years apart, so that each child's individuality can be well defined before he or she has to "share" the mother's attention.

There are no easy answers. However, the more aware we are of the child's special needs during development, the better we can plan to meet those needs. If we can meet enough of these needs, we will raise children to be independent, loving adults who will not be endangered in relationships, but who will thrive in them.

Sources

Adams, Paul L., and Fras, Ivan, *Beginning Child Psychiatry*. New York: Brunner/Mazel, 1988, 299–309.

Adler, Gerald, "Hospital Management of Borderline Patients and Its Relation to Psychotherapy." In *Borderline Personality Disorders: The Concept, the Syndrome, the Patient*, edited by Peter Hartocollis. New York: International Universities Press, 1977, 307–23.

Anonymous, "Day Care Dilemma Leaves Parents Pressured, Confused," *Psychiatric News*, November 4, 1988.

Berger, Philip A., "Pharmacological Treatment for Borderline Personality Disorder." In *New Insights on the Treatment of Borderline and Narcissistic Disorders: Bulletin of the Menninger Clinic*, 51:3, 1987, 277–84.

Bion, Wilfred R., "Emotional Turbulence." In *Borderline Personality Disorders: The Concept, the Syndrome, the Patient*, edited by Peter Hartocollis. New York: International Universities Press, 1977, 3–13.

Bleiberg, Efrain, "Stages in the Treatment of Narcissistic Children and Adolescents." In *New Insights on the Treat-*

ment of *Borderline and Narcissistic Disorders: Bulletin of the Menninger Clinic*, 51:3, 1987, 296–313.

Blos, Peter Jr. (chair), and Galatzer-Levy, Robert (reporter), "Issues in Psychoanalytic Treatment of a Borderline/Severely Neurotic Child." In *Scientific Proceedings of the Annual Meeting of the American Psychoanalytic Association*, May 18, 1985, 727–37.

Carpenter, William T.; Gunderson, John G., and Strauss, John T., "Considerations of the Borderline Syndrome: A Longitudinal Study of Borderline and Schizophrenic Patients." In *Borderline Personality Disorders: The Concept, the Syndrome, the Patient*, edited by Peter Hartocollis. New York: International Universities Press, 1977, 231–53.

Caulwels, Janice M., "Beware The Borderline." Letter to the Editor, *New York Times*, November 27, 1987.

Chiland, Colette, and Lebovici, Serge, "Borderline or Prepsychotic Conditions in Childhood—A French Point of View." In *Borderline Personality Disorders: The Concept, the Syndrome, the Patient*, edited by Peter Hartocollis. New York: International Universities Press, 1977, 143–54.

Cowdry, Rex William, "Psychopharmacology of Borderline Personality Disorder: A Review," *Journal of Clinical Psychiatry*, 48:8 (supplement), August 1987, 15–21.

Crafoord, Clarence, "Day Hospital Treatment for Borderline Patients: The Institution as Transitional Object." In *Borderline Personality Disorders: The Concept, the Syndrome, the Patient*, edited by Peter Hartocollis. New York: International Universities Press, 1977, 385–97.

Fraiberg, Selma, *Every Child's Birthright: In Defense of Mothering*. New York: Basic Books, 1977.

Green, Andre, "The Borderline Concept." In *Borderline Personality Disorders: The Concept, the Syndrome, the Patient*, edited by Peter Hartocollis. New York: International Universities Press, 1977, 15–44.

Grinberg, Leon, "An Approach To the Understanding of Borderline Disorders." In *Borderline Personality Disor-*

ders: *The Concept the Syndrome, the Patient*, edited by Peter Hartocollis. New York: International Universities Press, 1977, 123–41.

Grinker, Roy R., Sr., "The Borderline Syndrome: A Phenomenological View." In *Borderline Personality Disorders: The Concept, the Syndrome, the Patient*, edited by Peter Hartocollis. New York: International Universities Press, 1977, 159–72.

Gruenwald, Doris, "A Psychologist's View of the Borderline Syndrome," *Archives of General Psychiatry*, vol. 23, August 1970, 180–84.

Gunderson, John G., *Borderline Personality Disorder*. Washington, D.C.: American Psychiatric Press, 1984.

———, "Characteristics of Borderlines." In *Borderline Personality Disorders: The Concept, the Syndrome, the Patient*, edited by Peter Hartocollis. New York: International Universities Press, 1977, 173–92.

———, and Singer, Margaret T., "Defining Borderline Patients, An Overview," *American Journal of Psychiatry*, 132:1, January 1976, 1–10.

———, and Zanarini, Mary C., "Current Overview of the Borderline Diagnosis," *Journal of Clinical Psychiatry*, 48:8 (supplement), August 1987, 5–11.

Hartocollis, Peter, "Affects in Borderline Personality Disorders." In *Borderline Personality Disorders: The Concept, the Syndrome, the Patient*, edited by Peter Hartocollis. New York: International Universities Press, 1977, 495–507.

———, "Treatment Approaches." In *Borderline Personality Disorders: The Concept, the Syndrome, the Patient*, edited by Peter Hartocollis. New York: International Universities Press, 1977, 271–74.

Horwitz, Leonard, "Group Psychotherapy of the Borderline Patient." In *Borderline Personality Disorders: The Concept, the Syndrome, the Patient*, edited by Peter Hartocollis. New York: International Universities Press, 1977, 399–422.

———, "Indications for Group Psychotherapy with Borderline and Narcissistic Patients." In *New Insights on the Treatment of Borderline and Narcissistic Disorders: Bulletin of the Menninger Clinic*, 51:3, 1987, 248–60.

Hunt, Howard F., "Behavioral Perspectives in the Treatment of Borderline Patients." In *Borderline Personality Disorders: The Concept, the Syndrome, the Patient*, edited by Peter Hartocollis. New York: International Universities Press, 1977, 325–43.

Jones, James E., "Adolescent and Familiar Precursors of Borderline and Schizophrenic Conditions." In *Borderline Personality Disorders: The Concept, the Syndrome, the Patient*, edited by Peter Hartocollis. New York: International Universities Press, 1977, 213–29.

Jones, Stephen A., "Family Therapy with Borderline and Narcissistic Patients." In *New Insights on the Treatment of Borderline and Narcissistic Disorders: Bulletin of the Menninger Clinic*, 51:3, 1987, 285–95.

Kay, Rena L., and Kay, Jerald, "Adolescent Conduct Disorders." In *American Psychiatric Association Annual Review*, vol. 5. Washington, D.C.: American Psychiatric Press, 1986, 480–96.

Kernberg, Otto F., "Structural Change and Its Impediments." In *Borderline Personality Disorders: The Concept, the Syndrome, the Patient*, edited by Peter Hartocollis. New York: International Universities Press, 1977, 275–306.

———, "The Structural Diagnosis of Borderline Personality Organization." In *Borderline Personality Disorders: The Concept, the Syndrome, the Patient*, edited by Peter Hartocollis. New York: International Universities Press, 1977, 87–121.

Klein, Donald F., "Psychopharmacological Treatment and Delineation of Borderline Disorders." In *Borderline Personality Disorders: The Concept, the Syndrome, the Patient*, edited by Peter Hartocollis. New York: International Universities Press, 1977, 365–83.

Kunen, James S., "The Dark Side of Love," *People*, October 26, 1987, 89–98.

Linehan, Marsha M., "Dialectical Behavior Therapy for Borderline Personality Disorder." In *New Insights on the Treatment of Borderline and Narcissistic Disorders: Bulletin of the Menninger Clinic*, 51:3, 1987, 261–76.

Mahler, Margaret S., and Kaplan, Louise, "Developmental Aspects in the Assessment of Narcissistic and So-Called Borderline Personalities." In *Borderline Personality Disorders: The Concept, the Syndrome, the Patient*, edited by Peter Hartocollis. New York: International Universities Press, 1977, 71–85.

———; Pine, Fred, and Bergman, Anni, *The Psychological Birth of the Human Infant*. New York: Basic Books, 1975.

Mandelbaum, Arthur, "The Family Treatment of the Borderline Patient." In *Borderline Personality Disorders: The Concept, the Syndrome, the Patient*, edited by Peter Hartocollis. New York: International Universities Press, 1977, 423–38.

Masterson, James F., "Primary Anorexia Nervosa in the Borderline Adolescent—An Object-Relations View. In *Borderline Personality Disorders: The Concept, the Syndrome, the Patient*, edited by Peter Hartocollis. New York: International Universities Press, 1977, 475–94.

———, "*The Real Self: A Developmental, Self, and Object Relations Approach*," New York: Brunner/Mazel, 1985.

Menninger, W. Walter, "Introduction." In *New Insights on the Treatment of Borderline and Narcissistic Disorders: Bulletin of the Menninger Clinic*, 51:3, 1987, 228–30.

Pfeffer, Cynthia R., "Self-Destructive Behavior in Children and Adolescents," *Psychiatric Clinics of North America*, 8:2, June 1985, 215–26.

Rinsley, Donald B., "An Object-Relations View of Borderline Personality." In *Borderline Personality Disorders: The Concept, the Syndrome, the Patient*, edited by Peter Hartocollis. New York: International Universities Press, 1977, 47–70.

Rossner, Judith, *August*. New York: Warner Books, 1984.

Roundtable Discussion, "Treatment of Outpatients With Borderline Personality Disorders," *Journal of Clinical Psychiatry*, 48:8 (supplement), August 1987, 33–37.

Roundtable Discussion, "Psychopharmacology of Borderline Personality Disorder: A Review," *Journal of Clinical Psychiatry*, 48:8 (supplement), August 1987, 23–26.

Roundtable Discussion, "Current Overview of the Borderline Diagnosis," *Journal of Clinical Psychiatry*, 48:8 (supplement), August 1987, 12–14.

Ryan, Neal D., and Puig-Antich, Joaquim, "Affective Illness in Adolescence." In *American Psychiatric Association Annual Review*, vol. 5. Washington, D.C.: American Psychiatric Press, 1986, 420–50.

Sarwer-Foner, G. J., "An Approach to the Global Treatment of the Borderline Patient: Psychoanalytic, Psychotherapeutic, and Psychopharmacological Considerations." In *Borderline Personality Disorders: The Concept, the Syndrome, the Patient*, edited by Peter Hartocollis. New York: International Universities Press, 1977, 345–64.

Searles, Harold F., "Dual- and Multiple-Identity Processes in Borderline Ego Functioning." In *Borderline Personality Disorders: The Concept, the Syndrome, the Patient*, edited by Peter Hartocollis. New York: International Universities Press, 1977, 441–55.

Shapiro, Edward R., "The Psychodynamics and Developmental Psychology of the Borderline Patient: A Review of the Literature," *American Journal of Psychiatry*, 135:11, November 1978, 1305–14.

Singer, Margaret Thaler, "The Borderline Diagnosis and Psychological Tests: Review and Research." In *Borderline Personality Disorders: The Concept, the Syndrome, the Patient*, edited by Peter Hartocollis. New York: International Universities Press, 1977, 193–212.

Soloff, Paul H., "Neuroleptic Treatment in the Borderline Patient: Advantages and Techniques," *Journal of Clinical Psychiatry*, 48:8 (supplement), August 1987, 26–30.

Stone, Michael H., "Psychotherapy of Borderline Patients in

Light of Long-Term Follow-Up." In *New Insights on the Treatment of Borderline and Narcissistic Disorders: Bulletin of the Menninger Clinic*, 51:3, 1987, 231–47.

Strauss, Hal, "The Hemophiliacs of Emotion," *American Health*, June 1988, 61–67.

Sweeney, Donald R., "Treatment of Outpatients With Borderline Personality Disorders," *Journal of Clinical Psychiatry*, 48:8 (supplement), August 1987, 32–35.

Troiano, Linda, "Broken People, Center Stage," *American Health*, June 1988, 66–67.

Waldinger, Robert J., "Intensive Psychodynamic Therapy with Borderline Patients: An Overview," *Amerian Journal of Psychiatry*, 144:3, March 1987, 267–74.

Zubenko, George S.; George, Anselm W.; Soloff, Paul H., and Schulz, Patricia, "Sexual Practices Among Patients With Borderline Personality Disorder," *American Journal of Psychiatry* 144:6, June 1987, 748–52.

Index

Abandonment, 11
  behavior, 47–48
  during hospitalization, 106, 110
  and psychotic episodes, 29–30, 106
  response to, 21, 26
  by therapist, 115
Abandonment regressions, 114–116
  during therapist's absence, 116
Abraham, Karl, 9
Acting-out behavior, 25–26
  of adolescent borderline, 63–64
  to avoid stress, 55–56
  control of, 78, 111
  hospitalization for, 106
  self-mutilation, 68
  towards therapist, 115
  transference of, 68–69
  of transference feelings, 111
  see also suicide
Adolescent borderline, 41–43, 62–64
  eating disorders in, 61–62
  family therapy for, 89–90
  hospitalization of, 107–109
  self-destructive behavior, 63–64
  testing limits, 63
Alcohol and medication, 98
Alcoholism, 56–57
American Health
American Journal of Psychiatry, 46
Anger, 11
  against self, 27
  jealous, 27
  triggering of, 29
  use of, 27
Anorexia nervosa. *See* Eating disorders
Anti-social person
  symptoms of, 31
Anxiety
  medication for, 100
  in rapprochement phase of development, 37
Ativan. *See* Lorazapam
August (Rossner), 114
Autonomy
  of child, parent's reaction to, 39–40
  of mother, 39

Bergman, Anni, 35
Borderland (clinical term), 8–9
Borderline (clinical term), 9
Borderline patient
  depressed, 63
  early childhood patterns, 34–35
  employment of, 14–15
  empty, 63
  follow-up studies on, 120–121
  introverted, 21
  parents of, 39–41, 46
  pilot studies on, 60–61
Borderline Personality Disorder
  historical background, 8–10, 63
  origin of disorder, 12–14, 33–35, 40
Boredom in borderline patient, 11, 22
Bulimia. *See* Eating disorders

Carbamazepine, 98
Child care, 16, 123
  quality of, 124–125
Child development, 16
  awareness of here and now, 19–20
  darting-away behavior, 46, 61–62
  normal infancy, 35
  practicing phase, 35–36
  rapprochement phase, 12–13, 36–38
  shadowing behavior, 46
  see also adolescent borderline; rapprochement crisis
Chlorpromazine, 100
Clark, L. P., 9

Denial of reality, 23
Depressed person
  homosexuality in, 61
  symptoms of, 30–31
Depression, 20–21
  medication for, 99–100
Diagnosis
  criteria for, 10–11
  frequency of, 15–16
Diagnostic and Statistical Manual of Mental Disorders, 3rd Edition, Revised, 10, 60
Diazepam, 100

133

Dissociated speech patterns, 24–25
 changing use of "we," 25
Drug abuse, 57–58
DSM-III-R. See *Diagnostic and Statistical Manual of Mental Disorders, 3rd Edition, Revised*

Eating disorders, 61–62
Emptiness, 11, 20, 21–22
 definition, 21
 efforts to avoid, 55, 68
 and psychotic episodes, 29
Erikson, Erik, 42
Every Child's Birthright—In Defense of Mothering (Fraiberg), 124
Exploratory psychotherapy, 76
External objects, response to, 26

Family therapy, 89–94
 for adolescent borderline, 44, 89–90
 benefits of, 93–94
 identity of family unit, 91
Fatal Attraction, 48–49, 64, 65
Fraiberg, Selma, 124
Freud, Sigmund
 "armies," 34–35
 psychoanalytic technique, 76
Frustration tolerance, 55
 genetic tendencies, 34

Gender differences, 15
Good-enough parenting, 38–41, 123, 124
Green, Andre, 25
Group therapy
 borderline patient in, 87–89
Gunderson, John G., 14
Gunther, John G., 22

Hartocollis, Peter, 19
Histrionic person, 31
Holding environment, 77, 108
Homosexuality, 60–61
Hospitalization
 of adolescent borderline, 44, 107–109
 in crisis situations, 101, 109–112
 discussion of, 110
 during termination of therapy, 116
 long-term, 108
 organization of borderline units, 109–110
 patient's response to, 106, 108–109
 termination of, 108–109
 thirty-day, 107, 109
Hughes, C., 8

Individuation, 38, 50
 separation-individuation phase, 35
Interpretation
 definition, 83
 genetic, 83
 of past behavior, 83–84
 present focus of, 83
 therapist's role in, 82–83
 when to interpret, 83

Juvenile delinquents
 classification of, 63

Kernberg, Otto F., 38–39, 82
 availability of mother, 122
 on handling aggression, 113
 on supportive therapy, 75
 resolving the resistances, 85
Kreisman, Jerold, 18

Lief, Nina R., 15–16
Lithium, 98
Lorazapam, 100

Mahler, Margaret S., 35, 37–38
 individuation, 50
Manipulative behavior, 27–28
 to escape confrontation, 84–85
 in relationships, 51–52
 self-destructive acts, 67–69
 suicidal, 64–67
MAO inhibitors, 99–100
 rise in blood pressure with, 100
Masterson, James F., 40, 85
 adolescent borderlines, 63–64
 denial, 23
 good-enough mothering, 123
 practicing phase of development, 36
McClean Hospital, Belmont, Massachusetts
 pilot studies, 60–61
Medication
 antianxiety, 100, 101
 anticonvulsant, 98
 antidepressant, 99–100, 100–101
 antipsychotic, 97, 100, 101
 effectiveness of, 96
 interaction with other substances, 98
 introduction of, 101–104
 negative aspects of, 95–96
 patient's response to, 103
 risk of overdose, 97
 schedule, 101
 sensitivity of borderline to, 98
 symptom indications, 97–98
Mellaril. *See* Thioridazine
Memory lapses, 28
Monoamine inhibitor medications. *See* MAO inhibitors
Mood swings, 10, 17–18
 affective disorder, 98
 medication for, 98
 precipitating factors, 18
 and splitting, 19
Mother
 availability of, 38–39, 122
 self-image, 91
 splitting behavior with, 46–47

Narcissistic person, 63
 symptoms of, 31–32
Neurotic person
 symptoms of, 31
New York State Psychiatric Institute
 follow-up study, 120–121

Offer, Daniel, 63
Outwardly directed affects, 25–26
Overidealization and devaluation, 10, 20, 26
 of therapist, 71–72

Index ■ 135

Personality disorders, 8
   formation of, 33–34
Phenytoin sodium, 98
Pine, Fred, 35
Porcupine's dilemma, 11–12, 40, 49
Projection of badness, 29
Promiscuity, 58–60
Pseudoneurotic schizophrenia, 9
Psychiatric News, 15–16
Psychoanalytic Review, 9
Psychological Birth of the Human Infant
   (Mahler, Pine and Bergman), 35
   Psychotic episodes, 28–30
      medication for, 100
      triggering of, 29

Rapprochement crisis, 13–14
   and acting-out behavior, 26
   availability of parents during, 38–39, 122
   and fear of abandonment, 37–38
   need vs. fear of engulfment, 51–52, 106, 113
   in romantic relationships, 49–50
Recovery, 6
   age factor, 119–120
Relationships
   mimicking behavior, 50–51
   normal, 118
   with parents, 46–47, 92
   romantic, 47–48, 49–51
   splitting behavior, 46–47
   termination of, 29, 52
   transference in, 79
   see also porcupine's dilemma
Responsibilities
   of patient, 78
   of therapist, 77–78
Rorschach, Hermann, 9
Rossner, Judith, 114

Sarwer-Foner, G. J., 47, 111
Schizophrenic, 32
Searles, Harold F., 115
Self-destructive behavior. *See* acting-out behavior
Self-esteem, 19
Self-image
   in adolescence, 42
   essential badness, 24, 27, 29
   of family unit, 91
   and transference behavior, 29, 80
Self-mutilation, 11
Separation anxiety, 23
   in rapprochement phase of development, 37–38
Shapiro, Edward R., 39, 50, 73
Sinequan, 96
Single-parent families
   and Borderline Personality Disorder, 15
Some Practical Remarks upon the Use of Modified Psychoanalysis in the Treatment of Borderland Neuroses and Psychoses (Clark), 9
Splitting, 13
   and emotional shifts, 19
   essential, 18–20
   and rapprochement crisis, 38
Stable instability, condition of, 14
Stone, Michael
   follow-up study, 120–121
   structure, necessity of, 14, 54, 77
   in therapeutic setting, 77
Suicide, 11
   manipulative aspects, 64–67
   overdosing, 97
   percentage of borderlines who commit, 65
Support network
   in hospital, 106
   and medication, 104
Supportive psychotherapy
   drawbacks of, 75
   focus, 74–75
   and group therapy, 88
   hospitalization during, 108
   setting limits, 77
Symptoms, 4–5
   in adolescence, 43–44
   first appearance of, 14
   latency period, 43
   overlapping with other diagnoses, 9, 30–32
   pre-borderline, 43

Tantrums, 66
Therapeutic stalemate, 112–114
Therapist
   aggressive behavior towards, 81–82, 113
   changing of, 71–72
   idealization of, 71–72, 81
   patient reaction to, 78
   personal traits needed, 73
   responsibilities of, 77–79
   selection of, 72–74
   as Significant Other, 28–29
   transference with, 79–80, 110–111
Therapy
   optimism in, 75, 80
   reasons for seeking, 70–71
   regressions in, 78–79, 112–116
   setting parameters, 77
   termination of, 115, 116
   see also exploratory psychotherapy; family therapy; group therapy
Thioridazine, 100
Thorazine. *See* Chlorpromazine
Tidewater Psychiatric Institute, 5
Transference, 79–82
   of acting-out behavior, 68–69
   positive and negative aspects, 79–80
   with therapist, 79–80, 110–111
Trazodone, 99
Treatment
   types of, 73–74
Tyramine, 99–100

Valium. *See* Diazepam
Valproic acid, 98

Waldinger, Robert J., 46–47
Warehouse parenting, 15–16

Other Books Available Through the PIA Press are:

The Good News About Depression, by Mark S. Gold, M.D.

The Good News About Panic, Anxiety and Phobias, by Mark S. Gold, M.D.

Sixty Ways to Make Stress Work For You, by Andrew E. Slaby, M.D., Ph.D., M.P.H.

Guide To The New Medicines Of The Mind, by Jeffrey L. Berlant, M.D., Ph.D., Irl Extein, M.D., Larry S. Kirstein, M.D.

The Facts About Drugs and Alcohol, 3rd edition, by Mark S. Gold, M.D.

Crack: What You Should Know About The Cocaine Epidemic, by Calvin Chatlos, M.D. with Lawrence D. Chilnick.

Get Smart About Weight Control, by Phillip M. Sinaikin, M.D.

High Times/Low Times: The Many Faces of Adolescent Depression, by John E. Meeks, M.D.

Kids Who Do/Kids Who Don't: A Parent's Guide To Teens and Drugs, by Lorraine Henricks, M.D.

Overcoming Insomnia, by Donald R. Sweeney, M.D., Ph.D.

When Acting Out Isn't Acting: Understanding Child and Adolescent Temper, Anger and Behavior Disorders, by Lynne W. Weisberg, M.D., Ph.D. and Rosalie Greenberg, M.D.

800 COCAINE, by Mark S. Gold, M.D.

Light Up Your Blues: Understanding and Overcoming Seasonal Affective Disorders, by Robert N. Moreines, M.D., and Patricia L. McGuire, M.D.

A Parent's Guide to Common and Uncommon School Problems, by David A. Gross, M.D. and Irl L. Extein, M.D.

FOR MORE INFORMATION CALL
OR WRITE:
 The PIA Press
 Dept. BL
 19 Prospect St.
 Summit, NJ 07901
 (201) 277-9191

About The Author

Neil D. Price, M.D. is the Medical Director of Tidewater Psychiatric Institute, a private psychiatric hospital in Virginia Beach, Virginia. Dr. Price was born and educated in New York City. He received his psychiatric training at the Yale University School of Medicine, where he served as a resident and fellow.

Dr. Price has taught on the faculty of Eastern Virginia Graduate School of Medicine and has been published in the Journal of the American Psychiatric Association. He maintains a private practice in Virginia Beach, where he lives with his wife and two daughters.